HOUSEHOLD HINTS

HOUSEHOLD HINTS

AMAZING USES FOR
SALT, LEMON, VINEGAR, AND BAKING SODA

Heather Rodino

WELLFLEET

P R E S S

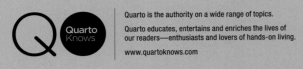

Quarto is the authority on a wide range of topics.

Quarto educates, entertains and enriches the lives of
our readers—enthusiasts and lovers of hands-on living.

www.quartoknows.com

First published in the United States of America in 2015 by
Wellfleet Press, a member of
Quarto Publishing Group USA Inc.
142 West 36th Street, 4th Floor
New York, New York 10018
quartoknows.com
Visit our blogs at quartoknows.com

10 9 8 7 6 5 4 3

ISBN: 978-1-57715-112-8

Design and Page Layout: Ashley Prine, Tandem Books
Editor: Katherine Furman, Tandem Books
Cover Illustrations, Shuttersock: sponge © Matviienko Nataliia; salt © DesignEvgin; lemon © Pensiri;
baking soda and vinegar © SASIMOTO

Printed in China

CONTENTS

INTRODUCTION

Walk into any big-box discount store, hard-ware store, or supermarket, and on the shelves you'll find specialized cleaning products for almost every imaginable task: stain-less steel wipes, granite cleaners, microwave cleaners, electronics cleaners, cleaners that specifically tackle hard-water spots or soap scum, products that remove sticky and gummy residues, cooktop cleaners, and even washing machine cleaners. We can freshen  our home with various sprays, candles, and odor eliminators that plug into an electrical outlet or get stuck in the toilet. When it comes to beauty products, the list is just as long, if not longer: Our bathroom cabinets are filled with toners, cleansers, lotions, scrubs, facial masks, blemish treatments, shampoos, conditioners, bath salts, bubble baths, deodorants, and more.

While it's convenient to have so many products to choose from, many of us have at least a nagging worry about the safety of these often-expensive items, some of them made with harsh, toxic chemicals that may not be good for our health, our family's health, or the environment as a whole. (After all, many cleaning products warn you to avoid inhaling the fumes, getting the product on skin, or leaving it on food surfaces.) And if you're at all like me, you also may be attracted to the idea of getting rid of some of that clutter and paring down your cleaning or beauty routine with affordable, time-tested, multipurpose products.

When I was first approached about writing *Household Hints*, I was a curious skeptic regarding the effectiveness of salt, lemons, baking soda, and vinegar in the

home. Sure, I had a box of baking soda in the refrigerator and I occasionally added a little bit of it to freshen up a load of laundry. But I wasn't sure if these humble items could do the job of most of the specialized stuff I already had. Even though I consider myself fairly green and eco-minded, I am also a busy professional, so I confess it seemed so much easier to buy products all ready for use, rather than mixing up my own concoctions.

As I started getting deeper into my research I realized there was only one way to find out how well these products worked—try them! Could baking soda really be as effective at exfoliating my face as my fancy department-store scrub? (Yes, maybe even more so.) Could I, once and for all, eliminate the hard-water stains on my long-suffering glass shower door and bathroom tile with a mix of vinegar and dish soap? (Yes.) Would vinegar and baking soda clear my drain as well as the brand-that-shall-not-be-named that I often resorted to in desperation? (Well, almost.)

One of the first tips I tried was a familiar one: to clean the buildup in my electric teakettle with vinegar. I dumped full-strength vinegar into the bottom and came back fifteen minutes later. I could see the buildup was nearly gone, now swirling loosely around the bottom. For good measure, I filled the kettle the rest of the way with water and put it to boil. That helped remove the remaining scale. No need to buy that expensive calcium- and lime-eliminating product anymore.

After many such little successes, I gradually became a convert to the very real efficacy of these everyday products. I suppose my mom had always told me so—and some of the tips you'll find here are due to her—but I had to become convinced for myself.

So, if you have always wanted to be greener and more frugal around the home and in your personal care, but have never taken the time to do it, keep reading: This is the book for you. If you're already a veteran in this area, there's plenty here for you as well. From the familiar to the surprising, this book collects hundreds of time-tested home tips and well-loved folk wisdom. You'll see just how easy and afford-able it is to incorporate salt, lemon, baking soda, and vinegar—in often surprising ways—into your routine. Not only will we look at cleaning and personal care, but we'll also tackle how these fabulous four ingredients can be used to great effect in the kitchen. (They are, after all, foods!) In addition, you'll see how they can help keep your pet clean and spiffy-looking, keep pests away, and make sure your garden and yard stay in top shape. As a bonus, we'll look at other multipurpose prod-ucts like hydrogen peroxide, rubbing alcohol, coconut oil, castile soap, and more. You'll find general cleaning tips, home remedies, and spotlights on the best cleaning tools.

> **Good to Know:** When mixing together vinegar—or lemon—and baking soda, go slowly. The acid in vinegar reacts with the alkaline in baking soda, creating a fizzing, bubbling chemical reaction. Remember those baking soda and vinegar volcanoes from your school days?

While salt, lemon, baking soda, and vinegar are fairly gentle, and these tips have been carefully researched, please use caution and common sense, as they may not be appropriate for, or may react differently to, certain surfaces or fabrics. Lemon and vinegar are, after all, mild acids, and salt is abrasive. Check the manufacturer's cleaning recommendations, or try the tip on an inconspicuous area before using it on the entire surface. The same is true with anything you put on your skin or in your body. Try a patch test or check with a doctor if you have any concerns.

Now let's look at each of our ingredients in turn to understand a little bit more about them.

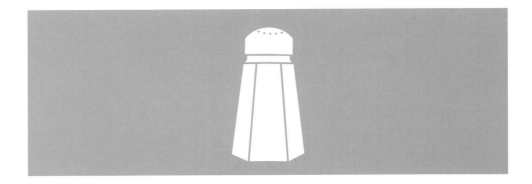

SALT

The salt that most of us use on a daily basis is sodium chloride, or NaCl, as you may remember from your high school chemistry class. One of the main sources of salt is, of course, the ocean, where it occurs in abundance, but it can also be found in underground deposits or even on the earth's surface in salt flats—think of the famous Bonneville Salt Flats in Utah, the Badwater Basin in Death Valley, and Salar de Uyuni, the world's largest salt flat, located in Bolivia.

Salt is essential to human health: It regulates blood pressure and helps muscles and nerves function properly.[1] Saltiness is also one of the basic tastes, along with sweetness, bitterness, sourness, and the more recently added umami. U.S. dietary guidelines recommend that healthy adults should consume no more than 2300 mg of sodium per day. Too much sodium can be a problem, particularly for those with high blood pressure, diabetes, or kidney disease.

Throughout history, salt has been of paramount importance in preserving and seasoning food, particularly meats, in the thousands of years before refrigeration was invented. While we now take it for granted, salt was once an important trading commodity and even used as currency. The word *salary* comes from the Latin *salarius* and *salarium* —"sal" meaning "salt." It's thought that Roman soldiers were paid partially in salt, or that part of their pay was earmarked for the purchase of the mineral. In addition, Rome had the *Via Salaria*, or salt route, by which much of their salt was transported from its source in Ostia.[2] Whole books have been written about the importance of salt in history, for its role in wars, taxation, funerary practices, and more.

In addition to preserving foods, salt is an abrasive, making it great for scrubbing everything from your cutting board to the dry skin on your heels. It's also essential in the kitchen, where the right amount of salt can be just the thing to make your food taste great. Pests like fleas don't like it, and it can also absorb spills and remove stains. Table salt or kosher salt are ideal for the tips in this book; table salt dissolves quickly, and kosher salt is great when a coarse crystal is wanted for scrubbing.

Kinds of Salt

While we don't have the space to cover every kind of salt, here are a few of the most common varieties and their uses.

Table Salt: A processed and refined salt, table salt is the most common variety, the kind you find in salt shakers. It typically contains added iodine, a nutrient essential to thyroid health, and often contains anti-caking agents to keep it from clumping. Most baking recipes call for table salt.

Kosher Salt: Another very common type of salt, kosher salt has larger flakes than table salt and does not *usually* contain iodine or other additives. Traditionally used to kosher meats, this salt is now the top choice of many chefs and food experts for everyday use in cooking.

Sea Salt: As the name suggests, this is salt harvested from seawater. It contains trace minerals and can vary in taste and color, depending on the source. Perhaps the most diverse category of salts for cooking, unrefined sea salt is a gourmet favorite as a "finishing salt," when you want to add a few flakes at the end of the cooking process to taste and appreciate the uniqueness of it. Sprinkle it on meats, eggs, vegetables, even desserts. The very flaky Maldon salt from England is delicious and generally easy to find. *Fleur de sel*, or "flower of salt," is a high-quality, hand-harvested sea salt, traditionally from France, but also produced in other countries. *Sel gris*, or grey salt, is a moist, coarse, and mineral-tasting salt harvested from the bottom of a salt pan (an artificial pond used to extract salt from sea water). Hawaiian sea salt can be red, from being mixed with volcanic clay, or black, from being mixed with charcoal. Prices for these unique sea salts can go from the affordable to the extremely expensive. Many artisanal producers advertise them as having particular health benefits, due to the trace minerals and the fact that they're unprocessed, but medical experts often debate these claims.[3]

Pickling Salt: Not surprisingly, pickling salt is your choice for canning and pickling recipes. It does not contain iodine or anti-caking agents. An additive-free kosher salt is an acceptable substitute for pickling salt.

Epsom Salt: Epsom salt is not true salt, but magnesium sulfate. Epsom salt has many cleaning, health, and beauty uses. See the sidebar on page 207 for more information.

LEMON

The bright yellow citrus fruit known as the lemon is thought to have originated somewhere in southeast Asia, perhaps India, but its use has spread all over the world. Lemons have been widely used in the Middle East for more than a thousand years. Christopher Columbus brought seeds from Europe to Hispaniola in his 1493 voyage. Several hundred years later, in the eighteenth century, the British navy began giving sailors lemon juice when it was noticed it prevented scurvy (thanks to the high vitamin C content).[4]

The culinary uses of lemon—both juice and zest—are endless. On the sweet side, there's lemon curd, lemon meringue pie, and lemon bars, while savory recipes include lemon chicken and preserved lemon tagine, avgolemono, and lemon potatoes. To drink, there's lemonade, limoncello, or lemon vodka. In addition, lemon is fabulous in a supporting role, accenting and brightening the flavor of fruits and vegetables, fish, and meat.

In the home, lemons can disinfect, clean, cut through grease, and remove stains and rust. They can also deodorize with a comforting scent that is pleasing to most. For personal care, lemons can be used to bleach hair, exfoliate skin, and lighten age spots. For health, lemons can help treat colds and improve digestion.

While there are numerous varieties of lemons, the ones you'll most commonly find in the supermarket are Lisbon, Eureka, and Bearss.[5] Any of these are appropriate for the tips in this book. Meyer lemon, a gourmet variety with a mild, somewhat floral or herbal taste, is likely a cross between a lemon and either a mandarin or an orange. It's more expensive, harder to find, and best reserved for special cooking uses, not cleaning.

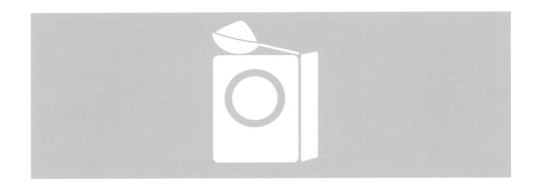

BAKING SODA

Sodium bicarbonate, better known as baking soda or bicarb, is a mild alkaline, which is why it reacts when it comes in contact with an acid like lemon or vinegar. It is often mined from trona ore, a natural compound that is then processed with carbon dioxide to form baking soda, but it can be produced synthetically as well.[6] (Fun fact: Wyoming has the world's largest deposit of trona, according to the Wyoming State Geologic Survey.)

In the kitchen, baking soda may seem more limited in use than salt, lemon, and vinegar, but what it does is of great importance: leavening. And don't confuse it with baking powder: See the sidebar on page 136 to understand the difference.

Baking soda is most often used in recipes for quick breads, cookies, and cakes, usually in conjunction with an acid like buttermilk or lemon. It can also neutralize acidity in foods like tomato sauce or soften bitter tannins in tea.

Where baking soda really shines is in the multifold applications for cleaning, deodorizing, health, and beauty. It doesn't just cover up odors, it neutralizes them,[7] so it's ideal for making everything from your refrigerator to your closet smell fresher. It's a mild abrasive and can both whiten your teeth and scour your oven. It can also exfoliate the skin, remove buildup from your scalp, clean carpets, make your pet smell better, and balance the pH of your pool. Baking soda can handle almost every cleaning task, though it may not be able to get your kids to pick up after themselves.

Since baking soda is always sodium bicarbonate, you can buy whichever brand you prefer.

VINEGAR

Vinegar is a fermented, sour liquid that contains acetic acid and water, among other components. It can be made from anything that has sugar in it, including fruits (particularly apples), wines, and cereal grains like rice or barley. It is created through a two-step process, in which the sugar is first converted to alcohol and then to acetic acid.[8] Most vinegars for home use have an acidity of about 5 percent. You may encounter something called "cleaning vinegar" in the supermarket; it has a slightly higher acidity. Experiment with it if you like, but most tips in this book were written with regular-strength vinegar in mind.

Vinegar has long been used to preserve foods, including fruits and vegetables (think pickles and olives) and meats and fish (pork and pickled herring). It is indispensable in flavoring foods, salads most of all. Studies have shown vinegar's effectiveness as a disinfectant and antimicrobial, particularly at higher concentrations, though regular concentrations should be able to tackle many household germs.[9] The Centers for Disease Control and Prevention also says that undiluted vinegar is effective in killing *E. coli* and *S.* Typhi.[10]

Vinegar, particularly white vinegar, has long been used as an all-purpose cleaning agent, from windows and floors to bathrooms and drains. It can even be used as a fabric softener. Vinegar does have a strong odor, so it may surprise you to learn that it's also a deodorizer. (The smell disappears when the vinegar dries.) For personal care, vinegar can be used to tone skin, eliminate product buildup in hair, fight body odor, and prevent swimmer's ear.

Most of the tips in this book use white or apple cider vinegar, but feel free to explore other types for cooking.

Kinds of Vinegar

White Vinegar: Made from fermented grains—often corn—distilled white vinegar is the workhorse and star of the green cleaner's toolkit. It is clear in appearance.

Rice Vinegar: Created from fermented rice, rice vinegar has a mild flavor and is used frequently in Asian dishes.

Malt Vinegar: Made from barley malt syrup, malt vinegar is essential to fish and chips and other savory food preparations. It is also one of the few types of vinegar that is not gluten-free.

Apple Cider Vinegar: The amber-colored apple cider vinegar is arguably the second most popular vinegar choice for cleaning and household use. It is made from cider or apple must. Apple cider vinegars that are unpasteurized and unfiltered can be found in health-food stores and are thought to have numerous health benefits.

Balsamic Vinegar: True balsamic vinegar from Modena, Italy, is made from grape must, not wine. It is aged for twelve years in wooden barrels and can cost as much as several hundred dollars for a small bottle.[11] Younger, less expensive varieties that don't meet all of the stringent criteria are available: to find a good one that fits your budget, look for the term "must" or "grape must" on the ingredients list, and avoid anything with caramel color.

Wine Vinegar: As the name suggests, this is vinegar made from wine. It's a diverse category of vinegars that are perfect for cooking and flavoring foods. Red and white wine vinegar are two of the most popular, but sherry and champagne are also excellent. If you want to get fancy and specialized, you can even buy vinegar made from specific varietals like chardonnay, muscadet, and zinfandel.

- CHAPTER 1 -
CLEANING

IT'S NO SURPRISE that the first and largest chapter of this book is on cleaning. As cleaning agents, baking soda, vinegar, salt, and lemon are virtually unparalleled, and there's little these four mighty—and frugal—superheroes can't do either alone or in tandem. For example, vinegar can leave your drinking glasses spot-free, clean windows, clear a clogged drain, replace your fabric softener, and clean your tile floor or your toilet. Baking soda can deodorize laundry, soften water, act as a scouring powder, get your oven clean, and freshen up your mattress. Lemons can clean your cheese grater, gently bleach stains, cut through tough grease, and fight mold in the dehumidifier. Salt is great as an abrasive, but it can also fight mildew, clean cutting boards, and even eliminate some stains, such as wine.

This chapter is arranged by area of the house. There are dozens of tips for the kitchen, bathroom, bedroom, laundry room, basement, and more. You'll also discover natural solutions for tackling floors, windows, and walls, as well as simple suggestions for keeping furniture and appliances in top shape. As an added bonus, you'll probably be surprised at how easy it is to pare down the number of cleaning products—and by extension the number of chemicals—you use in the home because of the versatility of these ingredients. And finally, you'll discover some clever (non-cleaning) household tricks and repairs.

A few words of common sense are in order though. Always use caution. If you're not certain a tip is appropriate for your particular surface or fabric, try a patch test first on an inconspicuous area, or check the manufacturer's recommendations. While baking soda, vinegar, salt, and lemon are fairly gentle as cleaning products go, they're not ideal for every circumstance. For instance, acids like lemon and vinegar are generally no-nos on surfaces like granite and marble and fine fabrics like rayon and silk. And baking soda is not a good match for aluminum.

While cleaning may not be everyone's idea of a good time, there is something incredibly satisfying about being able to do it in a way that minimizes your environmental impact, is safer for you and your family, saves money—and most importantly—works! Let's get started.

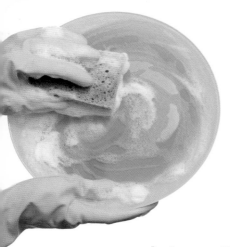

KITCHEN

Washing Dishes/ Dishwasher

 BRIGHTEN GLASSWARE

To keep your glasses from developing a whitish cast due to mineral buildup, give them an occasional vinegar bath. Fill the sink with soapy dishwater—as you would normally to wash dishes—then add in a good glug of vinegar. Wash, rinse, and dry your glasses, and you'll keep them looking new. For glasses that are already covered with buildup, soak them in straight vinegar, then wash and dry.

 NO MORE SPOTTY GLASSES

If you have a dishwasher, simply add a few tablespoons of vinegar to the rinse cycle to avoid unsightly water spots on your glasses.

 DISHWASHER CLEANER

To clean your dishwasher, run it empty on a hot cycle with a cup or two of vinegar. It will help eliminate mineral deposits and other buildup like grease and detergent residue. **Try This Twist:** Similarly, you can run your dishwasher empty with a cup of baking soda to help eliminate odors.

DEGLAZE A MESSY PAN

You tried searing chicken breasts in your favorite stainless steel skillet, but you flipped the poultry before it was ready, leaving a mess of stuck-on food that later burned. What to do? This cleaning technique takes its cue from the process of making a pan sauce, which naturally loosens food from a pan—often with wine or another deglazing agent. In this case, you'll use diluted vinegar. After you remove the food, and while the pan is still very hot, slowly pour in a 50:50 vinegar-water mixture to the bottom of the pan. It will bubble away (if it doesn't, return the pan to low heat). With a wooden spoon, start to scrape the bottom of the pan. You'll see that you'll easily be able to dislodge the food. After the pan cools, dump the vinegar mixture and wash as usual. **Bonus tip:** You can even try this tip with plain water.

SIMPLIFY SOAKING

Caked-on food stuck to your pans? Pour in some vinegar and let the pan soak for twenty to thirty minutes then wash it in hot soapy water.

DISH SOAP BOOSTER

Eco-friendly dish detergents are great, but if you find that yours just doesn't cut grease like the conventional stuff, then add a little baking soda. Just a few tablespoons of baking soda in soapy dishwater can help dissolve grease.

 ### SCOUR A PAN WITH BAKING SODA

If you've got a really greasy, messy pan, sprinkle it liberally with baking soda before washing. Let it sit for a few minutes, and then go at it with a sponge and some elbow grease. Be sure to use a nonabrasive scrub sponge for delicate surfaces.

 ### DISSOLVE PAN GREASE

If you're scrubbing and scrubbing a pan or dish, and can't seem to get rid of an oily film, pour a little vinegar or lemon juice on it to help dissolve the buildup.

 ### CHEESE GRATER CLEANER

Your homemade pizza was a big hit with the family, but you forgot to wash the cheese grater right after using it, and now the cheese seems impossibly stuck to the surface. If you have an extra half lemon floating around in the fridge, use it to help remove the stuck food. Just rub the pulp side on the grater, and the acid will help dissolve the cheese, so that you can just wash it as usual.

    ### COFFEE AND TEA STAINS ON CUPS

Coffee and tea stains can make a perfectly clean mug, teacup, or teapot look dirty. Fortunately, you can take your pick when it comes to cleaning methods. Rub the stains away with a sprinkle of baking soda, soak them in a mix of vinegar and water, or scrub them with salt and lemon. Or mix it up and try baking soda and lemon, or baking soda and vinegar. Experiment and see which one works best for your mug.

BABY BOTTLE CLEANING

Baby bottles can be cleaned with hot soapy water to which you've added some vinegar. The vinegar will help the bottle brush dislodge any leftover milk and it will also inhibit bacteria growth, so you can make sure the bottle is completely clean.

 ## ELIMINATE LINGERING ODORS IN PLASTIC

If you use plastic containers to store leftovers, you may notice that food odors tend to linger in the plastic. To eliminate them, sprinkle the containers with baking soda and fill with warm water and allow to soak for an hour or two.

 ## FOR STAINED PLASTIC

Foods like tomato, and dishes that contain certain spices like turmeric, can stain plastic containers. Baking soda solutions like the one above can sometimes help, but you can also try rubbing the plastic with the cut side of a lemon, then leaving the container for an hour or so before washing.

 ## LIPSTICK MARKS ON GLASSES

Long-wearing lipsticks are great for keeping your lips looking fabulous, but not so great to try to clean from the rims of glassware. To remove it, make a paste of kosher salt and a few drops of water. Apply with a sponge and rub until the mark dissolves.

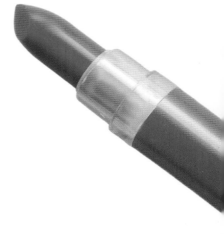

Sponges

SPONGE ODORS

To freshen up a stinky sponge, dissolve a few tablespoons baking soda in a cup or two of warm water and toss in the sponge. Let it soak for several hours before rinsing and wringing out completely.

SPONGE CLEANER

To both deodorize a sponge and kill nasty bacteria, soak the sponge in full-strength vinegar for five minutes. Rinse the sponge well, then allow to dry completely.

CLEANING REUSABLE WATER BOTTLES

If you've made the switch to reusable water bottles, that's great news. You also know that these bottles have one downside that the disposable versions don't: you actually have to clean them. If you're guilty of neglecting a water bottle for a day or three, give it a little extra TLC when you clean it. First, dump out any old water, then pour in a bit of vinegar and fill up the rest with water. Let it soak for ten to fifteen minutes to disinfect, then wash with hot soapy water and a bottle brush. Rinse thoroughly and allow to dry completely.

BE SPONGE SAVVY

The kitchen sponge, according to multiple studies, is the dirtiest, most bacteria-laden item in your entire home (yes, even more so than the toilet), and you use it to clean your dishes. Not surprisingly, all of those nooks and crannies harbor germs. Plus, the sponge doesn't often have a chance to dry out between uses, which means that the bacteria can multiply at an alarming rate. And if you then use that wet, smelly sponge to wipe your countertops, well, you're spreading those germs all over your kitchen.

So what's the proper kitchen sponge–care protocol? First, after every use, you should rinse it, ring it out completely, and store it in an area where it has a chance to dry. If you can, use a clean dishcloth and hot soapy water to wipe up countertops—not a sponge. Then, on a weekly basis, use one of the sponge cleaning tips below, and finally, replace the sponge regularly. Here's a roundup of some of the best sponge-sanitizing methods I've found.

Bleach: According to a 2015 Good Housekeeping test[13], if you soak a sponge for five minutes in a bleach solution of three quarters cup bleach to one gallon water, you'll kill almost all harmful bacteria.

Vinegar: If you don't want to use bleach, there's good news for vinegar fans: a five-minute soak in straight vinegar will kill *almost* as many germs.

Microwave: What about the microwave? You've probably heard that zapping a sponge in the microwave will kill germs. It's effective, but you have to be careful. To reduce the risk of fire, *never* stick a dry sponge in the microwave. Two minutes should do the trick for a wet sponge, but keep an eye on it and be very careful when you remove the it; the sponge will be scorching hot.

Boiling: The cooking and kitchen experts at America's Test Kitchen say boiling is the best way to clean a sponge.[14] Boil for a full five minutes.

REFRIGERATOR

 ## AN OLDIE BUT A GOODIE

When you think about uses for baking soda in the kitchen, the first thing that probably comes to mind is the refrigerator. And indeed, no book of natural household hints would be complete without this tip. Baking soda is marvelous at absorbing odors, so stick a box of baking soda in the fridge and replace it every three months.

Bonus tip: The freezer gets stinky too. Show it some love and put a box in there as well. Any brand of baking soda will do, but if you're feeling fancy, some brands make specially designed boxes for the fridge and freezer that come with removable side panels to expose a larger amount of baking soda to the air.

 ## FOR A CLEAN REFRIGERATOR

The next time you deep clean your refrigerator, wipe it down with a mixture of two to three tablespoons baking soda dissolved in a quart of warm water. Not only will this get the refrigerator clean but it will deodorize it and help remove stains. You can also use the baking soda solution to clean a frost-free freezer.

Bonus tip: A great way to clean drawers, shelves, and other removable parts is with warm, soapy water. Dry these pieces thoroughly before putting them back in the refrigerator.

OR TRY. . .

You can also mix together one part vinegar with two parts warm water and use this mixture to wipe down the empty interior of the refrigerator.

 REFRIGERATOR DOOR MAINTENANCE

Remove black marks and dirt from white refrigerator doors by wiping them down regularly with a baking soda and water mix.

 FINGERPRINT REMOVER

To remove fingerprints from stainless steel refrigerator door, sprinkle a little bit of baking soda on a damp sponge, rub the marks away, then buff with a dry cloth.

 LEMON-FRESH FRIDGE

Give your refrigerator an instant fresh aroma by wiping the freshly cleaned insides with a mixture of one part lemon juice and two parts water.

TRÈS EASY WATER TRAY CLEANER

If your refrigerator has an ice and water dispenser, it's a good idea to clean this area, because the water dispenser is one of the most germ-filled areas in your kitchen, according to a recent report.[12] In addition, the water dispenser tray—that small plastic item that catches overflow—has a tendency to get a buildup of water deposits. Just plain washing alone won't eliminate these marks. Instead, soak the tray in full-strength white vinegar for an hour, then remove the tray and scrub with a stiff brush and dish soap. Once you've rinsed and dried the tray, check it again to make sure the marks are gone. If not, repeat the process.

CLEAN AND DEODORIZE ICE-CUBE TRAYS

Plastic ice-cube trays can start to take on off-flavors from the freezer. Freshen them up by soaking them in a vinegar and water bath for a few hours, then wash with hot soapy water and rinse well.

Countertops

 ## CLEAN MARBLE WITHOUT LOSING YOUR MARBLES

Marble countertops can be a bit finicky. Because of marble's composition, you can't use any acidic product like vinegar or lemon juice on it because it could etch the surface. You should follow the manufacturer's instructions, but generally, diluted dish soap is recommended as an all-purpose cleaner. Inevitably, however, you're going to get a stain, and that's where baking soda can come to the rescue. You'll want to make a poultice—pretty much the same thing as a paste—of baking soda and water. Spread it on the stain thickly and cover the spot with plastic wrap for at least twenty-four hours, then remove the poultice and rinse and dry the area. If needed, repeat this technique. If the stain still persists, you'll likely need to contact a professional.

 ## TIP-TOP COUNTERTOPS

Depending on your countertop surface, you may be able to disinfect and clean with vinegar. Definitely skip this tip if you have marble or granite, but it should be fine for Formica® or laminate surfaces (to be certain, double check the manufacturer's instructions). Rub the surface with a cloth soaked in white vinegar, or if the smell is too much, dilute the vinegar to 50 percent with water.

 ## SCRUB AWAY COUNTERTOP GRIME

To clean caked-on or sticky food from a countertop, use coarse salt. The abrasive crystals will help dislodge the dirt. Rinse with plain water and then follow up with an all-purpose countertop cleanser.

Stovetops

 ## BASIC CLEANING

For most stovetops, the best cleaning method is hot soapy water and some elbow grease. However, if you're having trouble removing built-up grease or grime, try sprinkling the surface with baking soda and scrubbing with a sponge. Rinse the surface well with warm water.

FOR SCORCH MARKS AND STAINS ON
GLASS COUNTERTOPS

Glass stovetops can look sleek and elegant, and they are generally easy to clean, especially if you deal with stains and scorch marks as soon as they occur. But, if you're like most people, you might be tired after dinner and neglect a pan mark or stain and then cook on top of it next time, making it even harder to clean. While some of these stains might be permanent, others will come off, and the sooner you act the better. First, use a specially designed stovetop razor to scrape the affected areas. (You can find such a razor at a home goods or big-box discount stores or even in the cleaning aisle of your supermarket.) Next, make a paste of baking soda and water, apply it to the stains, and cover the area with a damp paper towel for about thirty minutes. Using a scratch-free scrub sponge, scrub the area thoroughly until the stains are gone. Rinse well with water and dry with a lint-free cloth. Stain still there? Try again, but this time spray a little bit of straight vinegar or lemon juice on top. Wait ten minutes, then scrub again. And the next time stains occur, be sure to clean them as soon as the stovetop cools.

 ## SPLATTER GUARD

When you pan fry or sauté food, small droplets of grease splatter all over your stovetop. To cut through this oily mess, mix together equal parts water and vinegar and use it to wipe down the stove.

 ## SALT IT AWAY

Sauces and other bits of food can sometimes spill on the stovetop while you're cooking. If you can't interrupt your recipe to clean up the mess, or if the stovetop is simply too hot to do so safely, sprinkle the spot with salt. It will make cleanup so much easier later on.

Range Hood

 EASY FILTER CLEANING

The oft-neglected exhaust filter on your range hood is a magnet for grease. That is its job, after all. While you're supposed to clean these filters monthly, if you're like most people, there's a good chance you might not remember the last time yours got a thorough washing. Turns out it's actually pretty easy to do. First, you'll need to remove the filters and fill the sink with hot soapy dishwater and a half cup baking soda. Drop in the filters and let them soak. Next, with an old toothbrush or other non-abrasive brush, scrub the filter, then rinse and allow to dry completely before reinserting in the hood. The combination of baking soda and dish soap will effectively dissolve the grease, making your filters like new—and ready to get back to work.

Oven

 TACKLE THE OVEN NATURALLY

While effective, oven cleaners contain some very harsh chemicals and it's understandable if you want to avoid using them in your home. Plus, the fumes are hard to take. Splattered grease from the Thanksgiving turkey and baked-on mozzarella from the lasagna that boiled over create a sticky brown or black film that seems impossible to remove. To get your oven back into shape, mix together one cup baking soda, one tablespoon dish soap, and enough water to make a paste the consistency of a thick pancake batter. (You can play around with these measurements or double them if you have a large oven.) With a sponge, apply the mixture to the inside of the oven. If the oven is really dirty, spray it with a bit of vinegar, which will start to foam up on contact with the baking soda. At this point, you can let the mixture sit for an hour or two, or you can start scrubbing right away. Once you're done scrubbing, use a clean rag and plain water to remove any excess cleaner from the oven.

SIMPLER VARIATION

Don't feel like mixing up an concoction? Before going to bed, stir together baking soda and water and apply a thick layer to the interior of the oven. Leave it overnight, and the next day, scrape off the dried baking soda, and then commence the scrubbing process on the previous page.

 ### GREASE-GETTER

So you've just cleaned the oven and probably don't want to repeat the task for a long time to come. For regular maintenance and to cut grease, wipe down the interior of the oven with full-strength vinegar whenever you get a grease splatter.

 ### DON'T CRY OVER OVEN SPILLS

Oven spill? Pour some salt on it while the spill is still fresh. The salt will both absorb the mess and reduce odors, and you can easily sweep it out when the oven is cool. **Bonus tip:** Use baking soda instead. Just scrub away the spill with a soapy sponge from the cold oven.

Microwave

 LEMON-FRESH MICROWAVE

Even if you're careful, the inside of the microwave can get covered with splattered-on food. (Here's looking at you, tomato sauce.) Plus, it always seems much easier to ignore microwave grime because you can—literally—just close the door on it. Here's a super-easy and classic way to clean your microwave. First, with a dry rag, wipe out any crumbs and discard. Next, in a microwave-safe bowl, pour about a cup of water (the exact amount isn't essential) and squeeze in the juice of one or two lemons. Toss in the peels too. If you happen to have a bottle of lemon juice instead of fresh lemons, use that. Just pour in a few tablespoons. Place the bowl in the microwave and zap for two to three minutes. Leave the door closed for five to ten minutes to allow steam to build up inside. Then, very carefully, remove the bowl from the microwave—it will still be hot. With a damp sponge or rag wipe away the caked-on grime, which should come right off. Dry with a clean towel and admire how the microwave sparkles. Plus, the lemon smells great. For a twist, next time, try using lime.

VINEGAR STEAM CLEAN

While this tip works just as well as the previous one, it admittedly doesn't smell as nice. In a cup or small bowl mix together one part vinegar and one part water. As before, microwave on high for two to three minutes. Leave the door closed for five to ten minutes to allow steam to build up inside, then follow the procedure on the previous page for cleaning.

 ## ELIMINATE STALE ODORS

Have you ever noticed how odors tend to build up in the microwave? You may be reheating your lovely cup of tea, but what you really smell is the extra-butter movie theater popcorn your daughter made last night. These stale odors can be rather unappetizing to say the least, but baking soda can help you neutralize them. In a small bowl or basin, mix together a few tablespoons of baking soda and a cup or two of water until the baking soda dissolves. Then dampen a sponge with the mixture and wipe down the interior of the microwave. If the odors persist, try placing the baking soda–water solution in a microwave-safe container and zap it for several minutes. Allow steam to build up for five to ten minutes, then wipe down as described previously. That should do it!

 ## FOR FINGERPRINTS, SMUDGES, AND DIRTY GLASS

To keep the microwave glass clean, and to eliminate smudges and fingerprints from the control panel, use a lint-free cloth and wipe down the door and exterior of the microwave with straight white vinegar. Rinse with a clean, wet cloth and dry.

CLEANING AND DISINFECTING GRANITE COUNTERTOPS

As any recent homebuyer or fan of home-renovation TV shows knows, the popularity of granite countertops has soared over the last decade. Granite is a beautiful igneous rock that can take on all different kinds of colors and patterns depending on its exact composition, so it's fairly easy to find one that will match your unique kitchen design. It's rather porous, so it's typically sealed when used as a countertop surface. It's also relatively easy to care for, but not as damage-proof as ye olde

Formica countertops. It's usually recommended that you avoid acidic cleaning products like vinegar or lemon. Also, oils left on granite can create stains. For basic cleaning, simple hot, soapy water is the way to go. If you're looking to disinfect the surface, there are plenty of pricey products on the market designed specifically for granite, but there's a much less expensive solution: just mix together half rubbing alcohol and half water in a spray bottle, and use it to wipe down your countertops. You'll notice that the rubbing alcohol will also give the granite a nice sheen. Why not give your homemade cleaner an attractive scent by adding a few drops of your favorite essential oils to the spray bottle?

Sinks and Drains

 ## CLEAR A CLOG

To clear a minor clog in a drain, pour about a cup or so of baking soda down the drain, then follow with about a cup of vinegar. This will create a foaming chemical reaction—remember those baking soda–vinegar volcanoes from elementary school?—so add the vinegar slowly in a drizzle and try to moisten all of the baking powder. Let the mixture work on the clog for about an hour or so before rinsing the drain with very hot water to flush the clog. Since this method is not as powerful as a heavy-duty drain cleaner, you may need to repeat it. If you have a drain that clogs regularly, consider using this method monthly as a preventative measure.

 ## DRAIN CLEARER

Out of vinegar at the moment and still need to unclog the drain? Don't fret. Another great method is to use one cup baking soda and one cup salt. Pour both down the drain and flush with very hot water until it runs clear.

FOR PRETTY PORCELAIN SINKS

Porcelain sinks can be beautiful, giving a vintage farmhouse feel to your kitchen, but they scratch and stain easily. Bleach-soaked paper towels are often offered as a solution, but if you're hesitant to use bleach on your sink, try baking soda and hydrogen peroxide instead. In a small bowl, mix together one cup baking soda and about a half cup hydrogen peroxide. It should be the texture of a paste. With a damp sponge, apply it to your clean sink and let sit for thirty to sixty minutes. Now it's time for some elbow grease. Scrub the sink well with the sponge until the stains disappear and the scratches are buffed. Rinse well and revel in your like-new sink.

 OR TRY . . .

Another approach is to spray your sink before going to bed with a hydrogen peroxide solution. Then in the morning, sprinkle some baking soda in the sink to cover. With a damp sponge, and adding a little more water as needed to keep it moist (but not to rinse away the baking soda), scrub the sink until it's bright and shiny, then rinse well.

  ## FOR SHINIER STAINLESS STEEL

Compared to porcelain, stainless-steel sinks are much easier to manage, but they can get a buildup of hard water marks and other stains. One of the simplest, least toxic, and least abrasive ways to clean your sink is with a simple baking soda and water paste. Scrub with a clean sponge, then rinse with warm water. To prevent the water marks from returning, dry the sink after each use. You can also wipe down stainless steel sinks with a paper towel or rag doused in white vinegar, then rinse and dry with a clean towel.

  ## SALT AND LEMON FOR SINKS

To brighten and clean stainless steel sinks, mix together one quarter cup kosher or table salt and enough lemon juice to make a paste. Using a damp sponge, scrub the sink well and then rinse thoroughly. You'll be surprised how clean it gets!

SMELLY DRAIN

Sometimes the drain can get that not-so-fresh smell. And sometimes you have an old box of baking soda in the back of the fridge that you're not sure what to do with. Here's a way of killing two birds with one stone. Just pour the baking soda down the stinky drain and flush with hot water. It will absorb the offending odors, and you'll have put something old to good use.

 SINK STAIN MANAGEMENT

To remove minor stains from a stainless steel sink, cut a lemon into wedges and rub the pulp all over the sink, paying close attention to the stains and those icky mildewed areas around the drain. Leave for an hour—or a bit longer if the stains are particularly stubborn. Rinse well.

 GARBAGE DISPOSAL FRESHENER

There's no better use for a spent lemon (or lime) peel than as a freshener for your garbage disposal. Toss it in and the blades will pulverize it, eliminating foul odors in the process. No citrus on hand? Try vinegar, followed by hot water.

 ## VINEGAR ICE CUBES

If you have a spare ice-cube tray, make a tray of vinegar ice cubes. Then toss a few down the garbage disposal to deodorize it. This tip is really a twofer because the ice cubes have the added benefit of sharpening the disposal blades.

 ## SALT CURE

Get rid of garbage disposal odors with salt. Just dump anywhere from one quarter to one half cup down the drain, then run the disposal.

  ## SNAZZY SINK FIXTURES

For tricky-to-clean faucet and other sink fixtures, mix together one to two table-spoons table salt with enough lemon juice to make a paste. With an old toothbrush and a little bit of the mixture, scrub the faucets (and other fixtures like the spray hose), making sure to get into all of the little nooks and crannies. Rinse well and dry thoroughly.

Around the Kitchen

 MAKE YOUR BLENDER CLEAN ITSELF

Don't let the daunting thought of cleaning the blender keep you from making delicious and healthy smoothies. After you've used the blender, rinse it with water, then add some warm soapy dishwater and a tablespoon of baking soda. Run the blender for thirty to sixty seconds to clean thoroughly, then pour out the dishwater and rinse well. This will get the blender super-clean and eliminate any lingering odors from the blades and other parts.

 REMOVE BLENDER RESIDUE

If your blender has a filmy, cloudy residue, blend together a few tablespoons vinegar with two cups warm water. The vinegar will break down the buildup and help neutralize odors. Follow up with a wash in warm, soapy water to make sure you completely remove the vinegar.

REMOVE STAINS ON FOOD PROCESSOR PARTS

If the plastic parts in your food processor become discolored because of ingredients like tomatoes, rub them with a paste of baking soda and water until the stains disappear. You can also try a paste of baking soda and hydrogen peroxide. The hydrogen peroxide serves as a mild bleaching agent.

 ## FOR FOOD PROCESSOR ODORS

Over time, plastic parts in a food processor can accumulate off flavors. To eliminate them, fill the bowl with warm soapy water and a few tablespoons of baking soda. Soak for a few hours, then rinse well.

 ## TACKLE THE TRASHCAN

Nobody likes to clean the trashcan, but you've more than likely taken out a particularly stinky bag and nearly been knocked over by the smell. That's usually motivation enough to deal with the problem. First, dump a quarter cup or so of baking soda into the empty can, then add a cup or two of hot water. Wearing gloves, scrub down the inside of the trashcan with the baking soda water, then dump it out, rinse, and allow the can to dry. As a preventative measure, sprinkle a little bit of baking soda in the dry can before inserting the next bag.

Bonus tip: Use a baking soda and water mixture to wipe down the recycling bins too.

REVIVE CUTTING BOARDS AND BUTCHER BLOCKS

Sprinkle a clean cutting board or butcher block with coarse salt (kosher is a good choice here). Cut a lemon in half and use it cut side down to scrub the salt into the board. Next, rinse any remaining salt-lemon residue from the board or block and follow up with a thin layer of food-safe mineral oil. This technique will eliminate odors, stains, and buildup on the board, keeping it looking like new for years to come.

  ## REMOVE STAINS FROM CUTTING BOARDS

You can also scrub away cutting board stains with a baking soda and salt paste. Mix together equal parts baking soda and salt, and add a few drops of water to make a thick paste. Apply the paste to a dry cutting board with a wet sponge, and use some elbow grease to rub the stains away. Rinse well with warm water. As an added bonus, the salt and baking soda will deodorize the board.

DEODORIZE AND DISINFECT WITH VINEGAR

If you've been chopping something particularly strong-smelling on your cutting board (hello, garlic), here's a great way to eliminate those odors. After all, there's nothing worse than chopping fresh fruit on a seemingly clean cutting board and having it taste like whatever was chopped there last time. After cleaning as usual, spray the cutting board with full-strength vinegar and let sit overnight. The next day, rinse and dry the board. The odors will be gone. Vinegar also helps kill certain bacteria that proliferate on cutting boards.

 ## SPONGE SOLUTIONS

Soak a smelly sponge in a solution of two cups warm water and a few tablespoons baking soda for thirty minutes, then rinse, squeeze out excess water, and let dry completely. Alternatively, for a little extra germ-killing power, you can substitute vinegar for the baking soda.

 ## CLEANING CAST IRON

Here's a classic tip you should never be without if you love your cast-iron skillet. If your eggs (or other food) get stuck and leave your pan a mess, sprinkle the pan generously with coarse salt, and using a non-abrasive brush and some elbow grease, scrub the stuck-on food away. Rinse the pan with hot water and dry well.

RESTORING CAST IRON

Whether you have an old, neglected cast-iron pan that has gotten rusty or you find a bargain on a rusty one at a yard sale or flea market, you can often revive it with vinegar. First, clean the pan with hot soapy water and an abrasive sponge to try to remove as much rust and dirt as you can. Then, in a large sink, soak the pan in a mixture of half water and half vinegar. Let it soak for at least an hour, and no more than four or five hours (any more might adversely affect the pan). Next, scrub it until the rust is gone. Now season it using your favorite method, and use the pan more regularly so that rust doesn't form again. Well-cared-for cast iron can last for generations.

   ## DE-GUNK THE TEAKETTLE

Whether you keep your stainless-steel teakettle on the stove or use an electric one nearby, you know that it's a magnet for kitchen grease and sticky buildup. In a small bowl, place a few tablespoons of baking soda and add a little bit of water, just enough to make a thick paste. Then, using an old toothbrush, scrub the exterior of the kettle until the buildup dissolves. **Try This Twist:** If the marks are very stubborn, substitute vinegar or lemon juice for the water. Rinse the kettle well and dry thoroughly.

   GLASS COFFEE POT

There are numerous variations on this tip, which helps to clean out the stains that accumulate in the glass carafe of your coffee pot. All variations call for adding a table-spoon or two of salt to a cool, empty carafe along with some crushed ice or ice cubes. You then gently swirl the salt and ice in the carafe with a little bit of water, vinegar, or lemon juice (depending on what you have on hand) until the ice is completely melted and the stains are gone. The salt is a mild abrasive, and the lemon and vinegar, if you use them, help dissolve the coffee stains.

 KEEP COFFEE TASTING FRESH

Drip-coffee fans know that over time, even the best coffeemakers need a little main-tenance to keep brewing top-notch joe. To keep yours in shape, you'll need some vin-egar. Fill the carafe with equal parts vinegar and water, and pour that into the brew-ing chamber. Place the carafe back in its usual brewing position, switch the machine on, and let the vinegar water run through. For best results, repeat this once more, then run several cycles of plain water to remove any vinegar residue. If the carafe itself is stained, rub in a baking soda paste, let it sit for an hour or two, then rinse. For best results, repeat the vinegar process monthly.

TELL LIMESCALE TO SCRAM

If you have hard water, you'll notice that with frequent use your teakettle gets a rough-textured mineral buildup in it. To remove this scale, fill the kettle about one quarter full with vinegar and the rest of the way with water. Bring to the boil, remove from the heat, and let soak for a few hours. Dump the water and rinse the kettle with several changes of water, so that your next cup of tea doesn't taste like vinegar.

   ## TAKE THE TARNISH AWAY FROM COPPER

Copper pots and bowls can be tricky to keep clean, but surprisingly enough you can polish them with salt and lemon. Cut a lemon in half and sprinkle the surface with a very fine salt. Rub the lemon half into the copper surface, and watch the copper regain its original shine. Rinse and polish the item with a dry cloth.

Bonus tip: Another common version of this tip uses a salt and vinegar solution. Heat one cup vinegar with one to two tablespoons salt until the salt is fully dissolved. Remove from heat and allow to cool until cool enough to the touch. Then with a clean rag, rub the mixture into the copper until the tarnish fades. Rinse with cool water and dry with a clean cloth.

IN-A-PINCH SILVER POLISH

A baking soda and water paste can serve as a silver polish in a pinch. In a small bowl, mix together one quarter cup baking soda and enough water to make a paste. Apply to the silver with a clean, soft cloth and rub until the tarnish disappears. Rinse the silver in water to remove the baking soda, then buff with a soft cloth.

TOASTER OVEN GLASS CLEANER

Over time, the toaster oven glass door can get cloudy, sticky, greasy, and just plain icky. To clean it, make sure it's completely cool and unplug it. Then mix together baking soda with a little bit of vinegar, and, using an old toothbrush, scrub the door until the stains are gone. Rinse with a damp rag, and allow to dry thoroughly before plugging in again. You might also find some of these marks on the removable tray, so feel free to use the baking soda–vinegar solution there, too, if regular hot soapy water doesn't help.

TOASTER MAKEOVER

To polish up the exterior of a metal toaster or toaster oven, simply use a baking soda–water paste and toothbrush and scrub the outside of the cool, unplugged appliance, being sure not to get any in the openings. Wipe down with a damp cloth to remove the baking soda, then buff with a clean, dry cloth.

  ## USEFUL FOR UTENSILS

Occasionally kitchen knives and other utensils can get small spots of rust on them. To remove the spots, mix together a few teaspoons of salt and enough lemon juice to make a paste. Scrub the affected area until the rust disappears, then rinse and dry the item.

VASE CLEANER

If you leave cut flowers in a glass vase for too long, they can start to decompose, leaving a slimy and stinky residue behind. To clean the vase, first rinse it well with hot water, then sprinkle the inside with salt and enough vinegar to make a paste. Scrub the inside well with a sponge and allow the mixture to sit on the surface for ten to fifteen minutes. Rinse out the salt–vinegar paste, then wash with hot soapy water.

 ## OR TRY . . .

If the glass vase is too smelly to handle right away, fill it a quarter of the way with vinegar and the rest of the way with hot water. Let it soak for an hour or two before attempting to wash.

 LUNCHBOX ODORS 101

Lunchboxes can retain food odors, especially when your child forgets to hand one over to you for a few days. Wash with hot soapy water, then sprinkle with baking soda and allow to sit overnight. Rinse out the baking soda in the morning. Store the lunchbox open to avoid trapping odors inside.

 CEILING FAN SOLUTION

A ceiling fan in the kitchen can be a great convenience, especially on hot days. The only problem is that the fan itself is not so easy to clean, because normal dust and dirt become virtually super-glued on with a layer of kitchen grease and grime. Vinegar can help, particularly for plastic or coated blades. (For more delicate surfaces like wood, check with the manufacturer, do a patch test, or skip this tip.) First, remove as much dirt as you can through dusting. (To be safe, before cleaning a ceiling fan, you should shut off the breaker.) Then using a rag, apply full-strength vinegar to the blades. It will cut through the grease, leaving you with a ceiling fan that looks like new. Wipe the blades down again with a damp cloth dipped in plain water and then dry.

BATHROOMS

General Cleaning

   EASY ALL-PURPOSE CLEANSER

For an all-purpose bathroom cleaner, mix together the juice of one lemon, one quarter cup baking soda, and one half cup white vinegar in a small basin. Sponge this mixture onto tiles, toilets, tubs, sinks, and more, then rinse well with warm water.

 DIY SOFT SCRUB

If you're looking for a simple and natural bathroom scrub, look no further. Mix together one half cup baking soda, two tablespoons dish soap or liquid castile soap (Dr. Bronner's is an easy-to-find brand), a few drops of your favorite essential oil, and enough water so that the mixture is the consistency of cake frosting. (The essential oil is optional; peppermint is a personal favorite for the bathroom.) For disinfecting and mild bleaching power, add one tablespoon hydrogen peroxide. Use this mixture to scrub the tub, porcelain sinks, and shower tile. Rinse well with warm water. **Bonus tip:** If you want a thinner formula to store in a squirt bottle, just add more water—and shake well before each use. You can also double or triple the recipe to make a larger amount.

BAG THE SCUM

To break up soap scum and other shower buildup, mix together this simple cleaner you can store right in your bathroom. Dissolve one half cup salt in one cup warm water. Next, add two cups vinegar, and place the mixture in a spray bottle. To clean, spray the tub, shower, or tiles and scrub with a sponge, then rinse.

SHOW YOUR RUBBER GLOVES SOME LOVE

Rubber gloves are great for protecting your hands when you clean or wash dishes, but it's often hard to get them to dry out between uses. To help dry them out and prevent odors from forming, sprinkle a little bit of baking soda in each glove after using. Shake out the excess. The baking soda coating will also make it easier to slide your hands in the gloves the next time you use them.

Shower

SHOWER POWER

Over time, mineral deposits can affect your shower's water flow, even blocking off the little flow holes. If you're patient and the deposits aren't too bad, you may be able to pick them off with your bare hands. But an even easier way to remove the buildup is with a toothbrush soaked in vinegar.

UNDER PRESSURE

For tough jobs, you'll want to get out the big guns, and this popular tip has been used for years. Pour a cup of vinegar or so in a leak-proof plastic bag (a resealable zipper bag is a good option), and then tie this to the showerhead. Let it sit for a few hours, then remove and let the water run. You'll find that your shower's water pressure is like new. Plus, this technique has an added benefit of killing the germs that have been lurking there for who-knows-how-long.

BACK ON TRACK

Tackle those mildew-filled shower tracks with vinegar. Depending on the layout of your shower, you can either pour the vinegar directly into the tracks (as long as it won't spill out and soak your floor) or soak paper towels in vinegar and place them in the tracks. Wait an hour, then come back with an old toothbrush; you'll find that the mold and mildew will easily scrub away. To finish, just rinse the tracks well with warm water, and you're set.

SHOWER DRAIN DEODORIZER

You may have thought of deodorizing your kitchen drain, but the shower drain can get smelly too. Pour one half cup of baking soda into the drain, let it sit for fifteen to twenty minutes, then flush thoroughly with hot water.

Glass Shower Doors

 SEE THE LIGHT

If your glass shower door has so much soap scum and stains on it that you're having a hard time even seeing through it, fix the problem with vinegar. Rub a sponge soaked in full-strength vinegar on the shower doors, allowing the vinegar to work on the affected area for five to ten minutes, then rinse.

 A LITTLE PREVENTATIVE MAINTENANCE

This preventative tip is only for the most dedicated of vinegar fans (who also have a little extra time on their hands after taking a shower). Spray the glass part of your shower door daily with a mixture of two parts water to one part white vinegar, then wipe away with the rubber blade of a squeegee.

 ## SHOWER POWER

Many people swear by this classic tip: mix together equal parts warm vinegar and dish soap (most versions of this tip recommend Dawn, but give it a shot with whatever dish soap you've got on hand), and use it to scrub your shower door.

Bonus tip: If you've mixed up a little bit too much of this solution, you can use the leftovers to scrub the shower stall or tub. Rinse completely because it does make the area very slippery.

 ## OR TRY . . .

A similar solution combines the same measurements (50:50) of baking soda and dish soap. Use that to tackle soap scum and mineral deposits on doors. Then rinse completely and squeegee the door.

  ## LOVE WHAT LEMONS CAN DO

Rub the cut side of a lemon over your shower door. For a little extra scouring powder, sprinkle the lemon with some salt to cut through the soap scum.

Bathtub

 RUB-A-DUB-DUB, IT'S TIME TO CLEAN THE TUB

To remove stains from a bathtub, sprinkle the surface generously with baking soda, then spray with hydrogen peroxide. (Alternatively, you can mix together a paste of the two ingredients.) Wait about fifteen minutes, then scrub with a damp sponge. The combination of the two ingredients will brighten and clean the tub. Rinse well with warm water.

 OR TRY . . .

Instead of spraying the baking soda with hydrogen peroxide, scrub the tub with a sponge you've soaked in vinegar. Rinse with warm water.

 LEMONY FRESH

Once you've cleaned the tub, rub the surface of it with the cut side of a lemon. It will help prevent soap scum, plus it smells lovely.

SALT SCRUB

Grimy tub? Try this tip. You'll need a few lemons and some coarse salt, like kosher salt. Cut open the lemon and sprinkle the pulpy surface generously with salt. Use this cut side of the lemon to scour your tub, adding more salt and replacing the lemon half as needed. The citrus will cut through soap scum and grime, while the coarse texture of the salt will scour the surface clean. Once you're finished, rinse the tub well with warm water.
Bonus tip: Some versions of this tip call for grapefruit, so feel free use whatever citrus you have on hand. It could be a great way of using up a fruit from the bottom of your crisper drawer.

 CLEAN YOUR JETS

If you have a jetted tub, you know how hard it is to keep the jets free from mold, mildew, and soap scum. Every once in a while, depending on how often you use the tub, fill it with warm water just above the level of the jets, add one half gallon vinegar, and turn on the jets to clean. It's a good idea to check the manufacturer's instructions to make sure this is safe for your tub.

  FOR BABY'S BATHTUB

There's no need to use harsh household chemicals on your baby's bathtub or bath seat. To keep it clean, sprinkle it with baking soda and use a wet sponge to scrub it gently. Next, spray it with a mixture of half vinegar, half water to help disinfect and dissolve any buildup or residue. Let it sit for a few minutes, then rinse well with warm water and dry completely.

Tile and Grout

 BAKING SODA TO BRIGHTEN GROUT

Tackle dirty grout with baking soda. Just apply a little bit to an old toothbrush and scrub away. For stubborn stains, mix together both baking soda and hydrogen peroxide. Rinse well.

Try This Twist: To brighten moldy grout with less effort, spray it with a mixture of one part hydrogen peroxide and one part water. Wait forty-five to sixty minutes, then rinse.

 OR TRY . . .

The same tip as above, but substitute a mix of one part water and one part vinegar. This mixture will help break up soap scum on tile as well. (Double check the manufacturer's recommendations, as some will suggest avoiding acids like vinegar on grout, especially if it's been newly sealed.)

8 USES FOR THE HUMBLE OLD TOOTHBRUSH

The next time you change your toothbrush, don't toss out the old one. Repurpose it—for cleaning. Few tools are as useful in keeping your home clean: a toothbrush's bristles are generally quite soft and nonabrasive; the head is small so it can get into the tiniest of spaces; and that long handle means it has reach and can stretch where your hands and other tools might not be able to. (To kill germs before converting the brush for cleaning, soak it in vinegar or hydrogen peroxide.) Here are just a few ideas for how to make the most of an old toothbrush.

1. **Grout brush:** No matter which cleaning product you use, the toothbrush can make the unpleasant task of cleaning grout easier because the compact head helps you scrub just the affected area.

2. **Scuff marks:** Loosen black marks on tile or linoleum with a few swipes of a dry toothbrush. Similarly, you can use a toothbrush to remove scuff marks from shoes.

3. **Faucet and fixture cleaner:** An old toothbrush can maneuver around a faucet or fixture much more easily than a sponge or rag, removing mold, mildew, and even water stains.

4 Nail brush: No need to buy a nail brush. To clean the dirt from under your nails, just soap up your hands and scrub with an old toothbrush. (It's a good idea to keep a separate clean brush for this task; you don't want to use a brush that contains residue of household cleaners or other potentially irritating products.)

5. Great for graters: Use a toothbrush to clean stuck-on food on cheese graters, Microplanes, garlic presses, and anything else that grates food in your kitchen.

6. Veggie scrubber: Loosen dirt from potatoes, carrots, and other root vegetables.

7. Stain buster: Use a toothbrush to scrub out stains that you've pre-treated.

8. Box fan cleaner: Remove dirt and grime from a box fan by using a toothbrush to clean the plastic grate. (Make sure the fan is turned off and unplugged, of course.)

Toilet

VINEGAR FOR A CLEAN TOILET

Clean and deodorize the toilet with full-strength white vinegar. Pour one cup into the toilet, and scrub well with the toilet brush. Wait an hour, then flush. You can also spray the outside of the toilet—the seat, lid, etc.—with vinegar. After a few minutes, wipe with a paper towel or a clean, dry cloth.

FOAMING TOILET CLEANSER

Instead of using a commercial scouring powder on the toilet, sprinkle it inside and out with baking soda. Let the baking soda work on the bowl for about thirty minutes, then spray the toilet with a bit of vinegar to create a foaming cleanser. Scrub the inside well with a toilet brush, then flush. Use a damp sponge to clean the outside, then rinse away the excess.

 ## FRESHEN THE TOILET

Instead of buying one of those toilet air fresheners, sprinkle a cup of baking soda into the tank before going to bed. When you get up in the morning, all you need to do is flush for a clean, deodorized toilet.

 ## THE BAKING SODA BOWL

No need to buy toilet cleaner: just use baking soda. Add one half cup to the bowl, scrub well with a toilet brush, and let sit twenty to thirty minutes before flushing.

Sinks

 DISSOLVE MINERAL DEPOSITS

Even if your chrome faucets and fixtures *are* clean, they don't necessarily *look* clean if they're covered with water marks and mineral deposits. Here's a great tip to use on fixtures that won't be damaged by acids. Soak a paper towel in white vinegar and wrap it around the faucet. Check it after fifteen to thirty minutes. At this point, you may want to use an old toothbrush to help loosen the stains. If the marks are still there, wait another thirty minutes, then rinse and dry the faucet completely. The vinegar will help dissolve those unsightly marks, so that your faucet looks brand new. (It may be a pain, but the best way to prevent these marks from appearing in the first place is to dry your faucet anytime it gets wet.)

 OR TRY . . .

The same tip as above, but substitute lemon juice for the vinegar. It smells great and will have the same effect. Be sure to rinse away the lemon, and then dry the faucet with a clean, lint-free cloth.

DRAIN FRESHENER

One of the germiest spots in the whole bathroom, the drain is a virtual bacteria-fest. Keep it under control by regularly pouring some vinegar in it, then flushing with hot water after a few minutes. As an added benefit, the vinegar will keep the drain running smoothly as it helps break up soap, gel, and other personal-care product residues.

 ## UNDER-THE-SINK HELPER

Humidity can linger under bathroom sinks, thanks to steam from showers, damp sponges that didn't quite dry before they were stored, and more. To eliminate the stale odor created, place a box of baking soda in the cabinet under the sink. It will also absorb some of the excess moisture.

 ## TOOTHBRUSH HOLDER TIP

The toothbrush holder can get a little, well, gross. Between cleanings a milky liquid can accumulate in the bottom, making it seem none-too-fit to store something that you stick in your mouth. While you clean the bathroom, pour a little white vinegar into the base of the holder to disinfect it. When you finish, dump the vinegar and wash the holder in hot soapy water.

9 CLEANING USES OF RUBBING ALCOHOL

Often used as the active ingredient in hand sanitizer, the very inexpensive isopropyl alcohol—also known as rubbing alcohol—has numerous uses around the home. Here are some great ways you can incorporate it into your cleaning routine.

1. **Ink stain remover.** Ballpoint ink on fabric can seem like one of the most impossible stains to remove, but surprisingly enough, rubbing alcohol will take care of it. The key is to act as quickly as possible. Saturate a cotton ball with the alcohol and rub it directly into the stain until it disappears. Rinse the fabric with water to remove the excess, then launder as usual.

2. **Remove permanent marker.** Rubbing alcohol can remove permanent marker from hard surfaces like a wall or countertop.

3. **Carpet stains.** Rubbing alcohol can tackle ink, grease, and wax.

4. **Hair-spray remover.** Rubbing alcohol will remove hair spray from a mirror and leave behind a streak-free shine.

5. **Clean and polish stainless steel.** Remove fingerprints, grease marks, and more from stainless steel. Just apply a bit to a clean, soft cloth and rub.

6. **Remove stickers.** Rubbing alcohol will help take away the tacky residue that stickers leave behind.

7. **Disinfect phones.** Use diluted rubbing alcohol to wipe down cell phones and landlines. (Note that some cell phone manufacturers don't recommend using rubbing alcohol; check your owner's manual.)

8. **Clean eyeglasses.** Use a soft, lint-free cloth and a mixture of half rubbing alcohol, half water.

9. **Clean windows.** When added to a vinegar and water–based window cleaner, it can reduce streaks and speed up drying time.

Shower Curtain

 SALT SOAK

You can only ignore a mildewed plastic shower curtain for so long. To clean it, take it down and soak it in a bucket of salt water for an hour or two. If any stains remain, remove them with vinegar or lemon juice. Ideally, for best results, you should hang the clean shower curtain outside in the sun to dry.

 PREVENT MOLD AND MILDEW

Keep your plastic shower curtain in great shape by spraying it regularly with a 50:50 mixture of vinegar and water. The vinegar will help stop mold and mildew from taking hold in the first place.

 CURTAIN CLEANSER

Clean your shower curtain with a thin solution of half baking soda and half water. Apply the mixture with a wet sponge, then rinse it off with warm water. If needed, use a scrub brush to remove stains. The baking soda will also eliminate any off odors.

LIVING ROOM

Furniture and Molding

  COFFEE TABLE CLEANER

A glass coffee table can look great, that is, until it gets covered with fingerprints, dust, rings from cups and glasses, and other marks. Get it clean with a little lemon juice. Spritz some onto the surface and rub the glass with a clean, lint-free cloth until it looks like new. No lemons at the moment? Just use diluted vinegar.

WOOD BRIGHTENER

Wooden furniture can get a residue over time, leading to a dull and flat appearance and even a sticky finish. To brighten it up, add two tablespoons vinegar to two cups warm water. Lightly dampen a soft cloth with the mixture and wipe down the wood until it shines again. The trick here is that you don't want to get the wood wet, so be sure to squeeze out the cloth well. Buff completely dry with a soft cloth.

> **Good to Know:** While this tip is safe for most varnished wood, you should test a patch first. Consult an expert for antiques or other valuable pieces.

 ## WATER MARKS ON WOOD

Somebody forgot to use a coaster (not you, of course), and now there's a water stain on your wooden coffee table. It's often recommended to try a paste of salt and water or salt and oil. In theory, the salt should draw out the excess moisture in the wood. Leave for fifteen minutes, then remove, dry the area completely, and apply a furniture polish. If these two options don't work, other home experts suggest everything from mayonnaise to regular toothpaste.
Take Care: If the wood is antique or valuable, consult a professional before slathering anything on it.

 ## DIY FURNITURE POLISH

This next tip sounds more like a salad dressing than a furniture polish. In a small bottle with a lid, mix together two tablespoons vinegar with six tablespoons olive or canola oil. Shake well until fully emulsified. Dampen a clean, soft cloth with this mixture and use it to polish your furniture. The vinegar will remove dirt, while the oil will moisturize and shine the wood. You can also play around with the proportions, as some people recommend a 50:50 ratio of vinegar to oil. Just remember to shake well before each use.

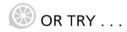 OR TRY . . .

The sweet smell of lemon. Follow the directions in the preceding tip, but substitute two tablespoons lemon juice for the vinegar. You might even boost the lemon power by adding a few drops of lemon oil.

Sofas and Chairs

 BAKING SODA FOR UPHOLSTERY

While most upholstery fabric can't be removed from your fur-niture and machine-washed, you can freshen it up without resorting to those artificially scented commercial sprays whose ingredients are a total mystery to consumers. Simply sprinkle your sofas and chairs with baking soda. Allow it to sit on the fabric for about an hour, then carefully vacuum it up. It will both eliminate odors and absorb oils left behind in the fabric. **Take Care:** It's a good idea to perform a patch test first.

 ELIMINATE ODORS FROM STAINS

After you've cleaned up a spill on your couch, sprinkle the area with baking soda to get rid of any lingering odor. Wait fifteen to thirty minutes, then vacuum up the baking soda.

 FIREPLACE GLASS CLEANER

Clean the soot from fireplace glass with baking soda. Make a thin paste of baking soda and water and spread it on the fireplace glass. Rub with a soft cloth, and rinse any remaining residue.

CLEANING TIPS

Dust from high to low. If you start with fans, crown moldings, and the top shelves of bookcases and work your way down to baseboards, all of the dust will fall to the floor where it can be swept or mopped up. After all, if you dust the end table before you do the pictures hanging over it, you'll just have to dust all over again.

Avoid "cleaner's block." Just the thought of spring cleaning can send some people back into winter hibernation. To avoid the crush of having to clean the windows, kitchen cabinets, and closets all at once, choose one "big" area or project to tackle per week, and make this your year-round MO. This week you might organize under the bathroom sink, next week you scrub the screens, the following week you clean ceiling fans and chandeliers.

Listen to music or catch up on podcasts. Try to make chores a bit more fun by distracting yourself. Folding laundry isn't so bad if you're hanging on every word of "This American Life" or "Serial." Mopping might be more pleasant set to the tune of Devo's "Whip It."

Keep your cleaning products where you use them. Why is your toilet cleaner under the kitchen sink and your furniture polish in the bathroom? Cleaning is quicker and easier if you store the cleaning products in the place where the deed needs to be done. You already have a box of baking soda in every room, right?

"It takes just as much time to throw something on the floor as it does to put it away." Perhaps your mom told you this too many times when you were growing up. It's not entirely true (it really takes no time at all to throw something on the floor), but Mom *was* onto something. If you put things away after you use them, you will save a lot of time straightening up later on. Plus, you can focus just on cleaning, not on organizing.

Deodorize with coffee. Much like baking soda, coffee is a deodorizer. In fact, if it's not tightly sealed, coffee can absorb odors from the refrigerator, which will affect the flavor. But you can put this fact to work, especially if you have some coffee sitting around that you don't like. Just stick a bowl of dry grounds in the refrigerator. Another use? Rub wet grounds on the hands to eliminate food odors.

Don't forget dish soap. Good old dish soap is an essential component in many of the tips in this book. It's a good choice for a green home because it's milder than most cleaning products, particularly if you choose a biodegradable eco-friendly version. In fact, dish soap is one of the few products that is safe for use on marble floors and countertops. For the simplest of all window cleaners, add a few drops of dish soap to a basin of warm water. Squeegee the excess water away for a streak-free finish.

BEDROOM

Mattress

 MATTRESS DEODORIZER AND FRESHENER

Whenever you flip your mattress (it's recommended you do so every three to six months for even wear), give it a little freshening up. Sprinkle the entire surface with baking soda, and rub it in with a dry brush. Let the baking soda sit for an hour or two, to absorb odors and body oils that may have accumulated over time. Then, carefully vacuum up the baking soda (along with any other dust or dirt) and return the mattress cover and sheets to the bed.

 CLEANING URINE STAINS

While a waterproof mattress cover may be your best friend when potty training kids, there's always a chance that somehow, somewhere, you'll have a urine stain to clean up. Mix together some vinegar and water and dab it on the stain to neutralize it. You can also sprinkle the surface with baking soda afterward.

 **PILLOW TALK**

Did you know that you should wash your pillows several times a year? Get them extra fresh by adding one half cup baking soda to the wash water along with the liquid detergent.

The Air

  PREVENT MOLD IN THE HUMIDIFIER

Avoid mold buildup in your humidifier by adding one quarter cup lemon juice or vinegar to the water mixture. (Check the manufacturer's instructions first.)

 ## A FRESHER CLOSET AND DRESSER

To keep your closet smelling fresh, store an open box of baking soda on a shelf. Change it every three months for best results.
Bonus Tip: You can also place sachets of baking soda in dresser drawers. Add a sprig or two of dried lavender for an elegant touch.

 ## CLEAN PAINTED FURNITURE

If you have a painted dresser or other painted furniture in your bedroom, you can clean it and remove marks with baking soda. Just sprinkle a little bit on a damp sponge and rub the area clean. Buff with a dry cloth.

FLOORS

Tile and Linoleum

 BASIC FLOOR CLEANER

For a simple way to clean tile and linoleum floors, add one cup vinegar to a bucket of warm water, and then mop. It will polish the floor and break up any accumulated residues—and as an added bonus, it won't leave any streaks behind. Rinse with plain water.

 OR TRY . . .

Another simple tile and linoleum floor cleaner uses one half cup baking soda dissolved in a bucket of warm water. Mop as usual, then rinse with warm water.

 OR TRY . . .

In a bucket of warm water, mix together one quarter cup vinegar, a good squirt of dish soap or liquid castile soap, and a few drops of your favorite essential oil (peppermint and eucalyptus are nice choices here). Use the mixture to mop floors, then rinse. The vinegar will dissolve dirt, the soap will help lift it, and the essential oil will leave a pleasant aroma in the air.

SCUFF MARK REMOVER

Shoes often leave behind scuffmarks on linoleum floors. While you can usually remove them with a damp rag and some elbow grease, baking soda makes the job a bit easier.

Hardwood Floors

 LESS IS MORE

It's not necessary—or advisable—to mop hardwood floors often. When you do, use the least amount of moisture possible to protect the finish. For water-resistant hardwood floors, clean them with a solution of baking soda and water. Add one quarter cup baking soda to a bucket of warm water. Using a mop from which you've squeezed out most of the water, mop the surface of the floor, then follow with a rinse of plain water. If possible, dry and buff with a towel.

Bonus tip: Baking soda can help remove scuffmarks from hardwood; just sprinkle a little on a damp sponge and rub.

Carpet

 ## CLASSIC CARPET TIP

Carpets can absorb all kinds of odors—from cooking and pets to smoke and spills. To eliminate them, use baking soda, of course. First vacuum the area that you want to treat. Then sprinkle the entire surface with baking soda. If it clumps, you may want to help distribute it with a soft brush. Now, all you have

Good to Know: For all carpet tips, test for colorfastness. Or check the manufacturer's recommendations for what's safe to use on spills, stains, and more.

to do is wait—a few hours is good; overnight is even better. Simply vacuum up all of the baking soda and the room will smell much fresher. And as an added bonus, the baking soda will freshen up the inside of the vacuum, which can sometimes produce its own odors. If you'd like to give a subtle aroma to the room, mix in a few drops of your favorite essential oil into the baking soda before sprinkling it.

 ## STAIN BE GONE

For a carpet stain, including a urine stain from a pet, blot the area well with clean towels. Then spray the area with a 50:50 mixture of vinegar and water, and allow it to soak into the fibers. Then blot again to dry.

 ## OR TRY . . .

You can also try a paste of baking soda and vinegar as a stain remover.

FOR GREASE STAINS

Rubbing alcohol is great at working on grease stains, especially when combined with salt. Mix together two tablespoons salt and one half cup rubbing alcohol. Dab this mixture into the grease stain until it's gone.

 FOR LIGHT STAINS

To clean light carpet stains, dissolve one half cup baking soda in a few cups of warm water and brush this mixture into the carpet.

MICROFIBER CLOTHS

While you don't *need* microfiber cloths, you should know that they *do* make cleaning a lot easier. Whether used dry, dampened with water, or sprayed with furniture polish, they're the bee's knees when it comes to picking up dust. Plus, they're lint-free and soft, so you don't have to worry about scratching delicate objects or leaving behind fiber particles. Unlike paper towels, you can toss them in the wash over and over again. (Though no fabric softener, please.) Some companies even make different versions for general dusting, stainless steel, electronics, and glass, so you can clean more effectively with fewer chemical products.

KIDS' STUFF

CLEAN PLASTIC TOYS

Plastic baby toys can pick up all kinds of germs and dirt. They're tossed to the floor, chewed on, and may even contain the remains of your child's breakfast. To clean and disinfect them without using harsh chemicals, mix together equal parts vinegar and water in a spray bottle, and spray the entire surface of the toy. Let sit for ten minutes or so, then use a clean, damp cloth or sponge to scrub away any dirt. Rinse well with warm water to remove any vinegar residue and dry completely before giving back to baby.

FOR BOARD AND VINYL BOOKS

You can also use the above spray to clean board books or those puffy vinyl books. Instead of spraying the book directly, spray a little of the vinegar mix on a clean cloth and use it to wipe down the pages.

 ## CLEAN DOLLS AND ACTION FIGURES

Dolls and action figures can get dirty too. Spray them with a vinegar–water mix, scrub, then rinse.

 ## GENTLE TOY CLEANER

Kids' toys large and small can be maintained with a simple baking soda and water solution. Dissolve one part baking soda in four parts warm water and use this to wipe down dolls, bikes, wagons, inflatables, blocks, figurines, and more.

FOR SPIT-UP ODORS

Neutralize the odor of baby spit-up with baking soda. Sprinkle some on the affected fabric and then launder as usual.

 ## SAVE TEDDY!

If your child has that one old stuffed animal that she can't live without, but you know that one more trip through the wash will certainly destroy it, try this tip. Dust the entire toy with baking soda, and let it sit for a few hours before brushing or vacuuming the toy. The baking soda will help absorb odors, oils, and dirt, so that that special teddy can hang on just a little bit longer.

8 CLEVER HOUSEHOLD USES FOR COOKING OIL

Like salt, baking soda, vinegar, and lemon, cooking oil—be it olive, corn, canola, or vegetable—is one of the most multipurpose ingredients in the home. And similarly, its many uses extend far beyond cooking. Here are a few of the best.

1. **Grease a squeaky hinge.** Do you wake up the baby—or even the downstairs neighbor—every time you open the bedroom door? Rub a little vegetable oil into the squealing hinge, being sure to open and close the door a few times to work the oil into the hinge.

2. **Don't get stuck out in the cold.** If you're having a hard time getting your key in your front door, the lock may need a little lubrication. Rub your key with some oil and stick it in and out of the lock a few times to grease it. You'll be able to enter your home with ease.

3. **Unzip in a flash.** A dot of vegetable oil on a stuck zipper will allow it to slide smoothly.

4. **Make a price tag disappear.** If you peel a price tag off an item, it often leaves behind a sticky residue. Dab the area with a little oil and rub until the sticky stuff goes away.

5. **Bye-bye, bumper stickers.** Saturate a bumper sticker with oil and scrape away. A little bit of soapy water will help remove the grease when you're done.

6. **Clean hands.** When working with a substance that leaves your hands sticky or tacky, rub them with vegetable or olive oil to remove it.

7. **Polish shoes.** Add a small amount of coconut or olive oil to a clean, soft cloth and use it to shine leather shoes. Buff with a dry cloth.

8. **Polish stainless steel.** Keep those stainless steel appliances looking brand new. After cleaning, place a drop or two of olive or vegetable oil on a rag and wipe down the stainless steel to give it a great sheen. Buff with a clean cloth to remove any excess oil.

WALLS

 ## BASIC WALL CLEANER

Walls are one of the most neglected areas of a home cleaning-wise, but they can be a magnet for dust, mold, mildew, and other allergens. In a bucket, mix together one part vinegar to five parts water. Using a clean cloth that you've lightly dampened with this mixture, wipe down the entire surface of the walls. If you've got allergies, you'll likely be surprised at what a difference this can make.

> **Good to Know:** This tip might not be suitable for all wall surfaces, including some kinds of paint or wallpaper. Check the manufacturer's recommendations first.

 ## AVERT A CRAYON CATASTROPHE

If you're a parent, at some point, you're probably going to be faced with some crayon on the wall. To remove, simply dampen a cloth with a little baking soda and water and rub it away.
Bonus tip: Baking soda can help remove other wall stains and can be great on backsplashes.

WINDOWS AND SCREENS

 ## VINEGAR IS FOR WINDOWS

No one really likes cleaning windows, but you can make the job a little easier and more effective with just a few basic items from around the house. First mix one part vinegar and one to two parts warm water. You can either put this mixture in a spray bottle or a bucket, depending on how many windows you're planning on cleaning. Next, grab some old newspaper from the recycling pile. Either spray the vinegar mixture on the windows or apply with a sponge. Then crumple up some newspaper and use it to clean the windows for a lint-free and streak-free finish. It sounds a little crazy, but it really works—and is a great way to reuse newspaper.

Bonus tip: If you're not convinced you want to try newspaper on your windows, know that coffee filters also work (though you'll go through lot of them). Two other good choices? A washable lint-free microfiber cloth or a squeegee.

WINDOW PREWASH

Really dirty windows? You might need to give them a prewash. Add a squirt of dishwashing liquid to a gallon of warm water, and use this mixture and a sponge to remove the worst of the dirt (as well as any residue from previously used commercial cleaning products). Then get them nice and shiny and streak-free with the vinegar-water mixture on the previous page.

CORNSTARCH-VINEGAR CLEANER

Cornstarch can boost the cleaning power of vinegar for windows. In a small basin or bucket, mix together two tablespoons cornstarch, one half cup vinegar, and three cups warm water. Stir until cornstarch is thoroughly mixed. Apply to windows and rub well with newsprint or a lint-free cloth until clean and no streaks remain.

FOR TOUGH JOBS

Another tip for super-dirty windows is to use full-strength vinegar to clean them.

BAKING SODA VERSION

While vinegar is usually the top choice for window washing, you can also use a little bit of baking soda and a wet sponge or lint-free cloth.

THE LEMON ALTERNATIVE

Don't forget about lemons. In a spray bottle, mix together two tablespoons lemon juice and one quarter cup vinegar. Fill the rest of the bottle with warm water, and shake well. This mixture smells a bit nicer than plain vinegar.

  ## PAINT SPLATTERS

To clean paint splatters from windows, heat a little bit of lemon juice or vinegar. Apply generously to the spot with a soft cloth, then rub until it loosens. You may need to use a bit of elbow grease if the paint spot is old.

 ## SCREEN CLEAN

If you store your screens in the attic during fall and winter, they may get a little musty, dusty, and dirty. Before replacing them in spring, scrub dirty screens with a mixture of baking soda and water. Then rinse and let dry before replacing in windows for the summer season. They'll smell fresh and let in the maximum amount of air.

 ## OR TRY . . .

Diluted vinegar can also help clean the buildup that accumulates on screens with use. Add one half cup to a gallon of warm soapy water, and rub gently with a sponge to dislodge dust, grime, and other particles. Rinse the screens well and let dry.

Bonus tip: If you have the outdoor space, cleaning screens is easier to do outside than inside, and a garden hose makes rinsing easy. No outdoor space? Try rinsing screens in the shower.

9 CLEANING USES OF HYDROGEN PEROXIDE

Hydrogen peroxide, or H_2O_2, may be better known to creatures great and small as that, fizzing substance that comes in a dark brown bottle and is used to treat cuts and scrapes. (In case you didn't know, hydrogen peroxide breaks down when exposed to light, so that's why it comes in an opaque bottle.) The Food and Drug Administration considers hydrogen peroxide an effective antimicrobial, and as it turns out, there are lots of other common household uses for it, including as a bleach and disinfectant. The following tips use standard concentration 3% hydrogen peroxide.

1. **Clean cutting boards.** After cutting raw meat, douse your cutting board in hydrogen peroxide. Let it stand a few minutes, wipe up the excess peroxide, then wash the board with hot soapy water.

2. **Clean countertops.** Disinfect countertops by wiping them down with hydrogen peroxide.

3. **Wash fruits and vegetables.** Instead of buying a pricey commercial produce wash, fill a clean sink with water and one half cup hydrogen peroxide. Add the produce to wash, then rinse with water.

4. **Clean the refrigerator.** Wipe down the inside of your refrigerator with diluted hydrogen peroxide.

5. Brighten grout. Spray grout with full-strength hydrogen peroxide, or mix together with baking soda for extra whitening power.

6. Eliminate mildew. In the kitchen or bathroom, use hydrogen peroxide to get rid of mold and mildew.

7. Bleach substitute. Instead of using bleach to brighten whites, add one cup hydrogen peroxide.

8. Stain fighter. Hydrogen peroxide can remove grass, wine, and other stains. You can also use it as a pre-treatment.

Good to Know: Since it does have bleaching properties, it may not be suitable for use on darker fabrics.

9. Brighten floors. Add a cup or so to a bucket of hot water and mop as usual. For stains, use a soft cloth and full-strength hydrogen peroxide. Rinse with water to avoid further bleaching.

BASEMENT AND ATTIC

 ## FRESHEN UP THE NEGLECTED ROOMS

Just like the refrigerator and freezer, the basement and attic can often benefit from a little deodorizing. Place an open box (or two or three) of baking soda in each of these spots, and change every few months to keep musty, damp odors at bay.

 ## TACKLE BASEMENT MOLD AND MILDEW

The basement is a magnet for mold and mildew. Spray walls and mop floors with a solution of one part vinegar to one part water. If needed, scrub the surface with a brush to remove the mold, then rinse with warm water.

Good to Know: Allow the area to dry completely; use fans and dehumidifiers if needed. This is an important step. After you've spent so much time cleaning, you don't want to give mold a chance to take over again.

LAUNDRY ROOM

Good to Know: Not all tips are suitable for all fabrics, particularly delicate fibers like silk and rayon. Use common sense and read labels. If unsure, test an inconspicuous patch first. Use only white vinegar.

 ## FOR CLEANER CLOTHES

Many people actually add too much laundry detergent per load, and the excess can linger in clothes even after they've been washed. To make sure that your clothes get their cleanest, add a few tablespoons of vinegar to the rinse cycle (up to one half cup). It will help dissolve detergent residue, making sure your clothes come out looking great.

 ## WE *DON'T* WANT THE FUNK

Even if you wash your towels regularly, you may notice that over time they start to smell, well, off. A warm, humid climate can be one cause, especially if the towels don't dry quickly enough between uses. But another reason may be a buildup of detergents, which can make the towels less absorbent. As above, one half cup vinegar added to the rinse cycle on a regular basis should help keep them in good shape. However, if your towels are in need of more help, try running a load (on the hottest temperature recommended by the care label) with just a cup of vinegar and no detergent. Then wash them a second time with one half cup baking soda. Dry as usual.

 TOO MUCH DETERGENT?

If you accidentally added too much detergent to your load of laundry, add one quarter cup salt to the wash water to tame the bubbles.

 POWER UP

Add one half cup baking soda to your wash cycle along with the liquid detergent. It will boost the cleaning power of the detergent and leave your clothes looking brighter.

SOFTEN HARD WATER

Hard water getting you down? Don't add more expensive laundry detergent. Simply soften your water by adding one half cup baking soda to the wash cycle of every load.

 ## NEUTRALIZE ODORS

Add one half cup baking soda to the rinse cycle of your washing machine to neutralize odors and keep your clothes smelling great.

 ## REFRESH DELICATES

When stored in a drawer for a long time, doilies, handkerchiefs, and other small delicates can start to smell a little stale, even if they're clean. Freshen them up by hand washing them in a small basin with cool water and a couple tablespoons baking soda. If possible, hang outside to dry in the sun.

 ## BRIGHTEN BRIGHTS

You obviously can't use bleach to brighten colored and dark garments, so use vinegar. Half a cup added to the rinse cycle will do it.

 LEMON BLEACH

The next time you want to brighten a load of whites that are looking dingy, add one third cup lemon juice to the wash cycle. It's a much gentler alternative to bleach, and it smells so much better too.

 PERSPIRATION

Over time the underarms of shirts can become yellowed and discolored with perspiration. The marks can be embarrassing, but fortunately they can be removed. Pour full-strength white vinegar over the affected area, then toss directly into the machine, and wash as usual.

 OR TRY . . .

Another alternative uses baking soda and water paste. Scrub this mixture into the perspiration stains, and let sit for thirty minutes. Wash as usual. This tip has the added benefit of neutralizing odors.

DEODORANT STAINS

Your favorite antiperspirant can leave the underarms of shirts with darkened, greasy-looking patches. To remove them, soak the underarms in white vinegar and launder as usual.

 COLLARS

Nearly anyone who lived through the 1970s remembers the ubiquitous Wisk detergent commercials that pledged to remove the dreaded "ring around the collar." Turns out baking soda and hydrogen peroxide will do the same thing. Use an old toothbrush to scrub a paste of the two ingredients into the yellowed collar, and then toss the shirt right in the washing machine. It's (almost) as easy as pouring the Wisk—and just as effective.

  OR TRY . . .

The same tip as above, but with a mix of baking soda and vinegar.

 ## FOR WHITE LINEN

Keep sturdy white fabrics such as linen looking their best with lemon. Gather together the fabrics you want to brighten and a pot big enough to fit them. Fill the pot with water, add one sliced lemon, bring the water to a boil, then remove from the heat. Carefully add your fabric and immerse in the water. After a few hours, remove from the water and wash as usual. Surprisingly enough, boiling linen is an old-fashioned technique, and the lemon will make the whites even whiter.

 ## SALT SOAK

To clean and brighten old linens, place the fabric in a bucket of water in which you've dissolved one half cup salt. Soak for twenty-four hours, then rinse and dry in the sun.

 ## REMOVE YELLOW SPOTS

Fabrics stored too long in a closet can sometimes develop yellow spots. To remove them without bleach, make a paste of baking soda and water and apply it to the marks as a pre-treatment. For additional cleaning power, add one quarter cup baking soda to the wash cycle of the load.

DE-STINK SPORTS GEAR

Sometimes, no matter how many times you wash workout gear, it can have an unpleasant lingering odor that—embarrassingly—seems to reactivate with the slightest bit of moisture. To eliminate it, make a paste of baking soda and water and apply it to the affected areas (say, the underarms), or if the whole garment smells, add one half cup baking soda to the wash cycle to deodorize. If possible, hang the clothes outside to dry.

 ## OR TRY . . .

Add three quarters to one cup vinegar to the rinse cycle.

 GYM BAG EMERGENCY

You just remembered that you left your gym bag in the trunk of the car—last week. And it's August. While your dirty workout clothes are sure to be fragrant, to say the least, all may not be lost. Prewash the items by adding two cups baking soda to the load, and allow them to soak for a few hours before washing. With any luck, you'll be able to salvage the clothes.

 WOOL WASH

Keep your wool sweaters smelling fresh. Most wool garments should be washed by hand (unless the care label specifically says you can put them in the machine). To eliminate odors, add one quarter cup vinegar to the wash water and allow the sweater to soak for a few minutes before rinsing well.

Bonus tip: Vinegar can help soften scratchy wool, making the fibers less irritating to your skin. It can also set the dye so that the color lasts longer.

FABRIC SOFTENER

There's no need to buy commercial fabric softener, when vinegar will work just as well! Just add one quarter cup or so to the rinse cycle and it will keep your clothes soft without clogging the fibers like the commercial softeners can do. Plus, many synthetic fabrics, particularly those found in microfiber cloths and workout gear like yoga pants, do not respond well to liquid fabric softener.

Bonus tip: Baking soda also works well as a fabric softener.

LESSEN THE LINT

It's a great idea to hang your clothes out to dry on the washline. Not only is it much better for the environment, but it can save you a bundle on your electricity bill because the dryer is one of the biggest energy hogs in the home. (Not to mention that clothes dried in the sun smell wonderful.) However, you may miss the amazing lint-gathering ability of the dryer. It turns out that a little vinegar added to the rinse cycle can help reduce lint. One quarter cup to one half cup per load should do it.

BLEED NO MORE

Everyone has *that shirt*. It's the one you dread washing because it seems to bleed like mad and color every-thing it comes in contact with. One solution to try is to add some vinegar to the rinse cycle. For some fabrics, particularly natural ones like cotton and wool, vinegar is thought to help set the dye—or at least reduce the color loss.

SAVE THE COLOR

Salt is also considered useful in preserving colors in fabric. To prevent fading, add one quarter cup to the wash cycle.

 REMOVE CHLORINE

The next time you wash your bathing suit by hand, add a tablespoon of baking soda to the water in the sink along with the detergent. It will help remove any lingering chlorine residue.

 NEW CLOTHES

It's always a good idea to wash new clothes before wearing them the first time. Clothes that other people have tried on can carry all kinds of germs, and the fabric can contain residues from the manufacturer. Add one quarter cup vinegar to the wash cycle of a small load to help eliminate those germs and chemicals, and wash at the hottest cycle recommended on the care label.

A LEAN, MEAN CLEANING MACHINE

To keep your top-loading washing machine smelling fresh and to eliminate any mildew or mold, run the machine empty on the largest, hottest cycle with four cups vinegar. For a tough job, stop the machine once it's full and let it soak for an hour or so, then allow it to complete the rest of the wash cycle.

BASIC STAIN REMOVER

For general stains, mix together a paste of lemon juice and baking soda. Apply the mixture to the affected area, let it sit a few minutes, and then wash as usual.

GREASE REMOVAL

To remove grease stains from clothes, first blot the stain carefully to remove as much of the excess oil as possible. Then cover the area with dish soap—a great grease-buster. Gently rub it into the spot, then rinse the area with full-strength vinegar. Wash the garment right away.

OR TRY . . .

Baking soda can help absorb a grease stain. Sprinkle some on a fresh stain and let it sit for fifteen to thirty minutes. Then brush off the excess and follow up with your favorite stain pre-treatment method, and wash the garment as soon as possible.

 FRUIT STAINS

You decided to have a healthy fruit smoothie for breakfast, but what you didn't bargain on was spilling the strawberry and blueberry drink on your brand-new white shirt. After you've dabbed up the worst of the stain, soak the spot in white vinegar, then launder immediately.

 JUICE STAINS

For dark juice stains, stir together one part lemon juice and one part water and soak the stain with this mixture.

  MILDEW SPOTS

For mildew spots on clothes, mix together salt and enough lemon juice to make a paste. Scrub the mixture into the stain with a soft-bristled brush, then hang the item in the sun to dry. If the stain persists, repeat this method, then wash the item as usual. Salt has an abrasive quality, helping to break up and loosen the stain, while the sun and lemon have mild bleaching properties.

WINE STAINS

It's all fun and games until someone spills the red wine. To treat a red wine stain, rinse the area with vinegar as soon as possible and then launder as usual.

 ## OR TRY . . .

As soon as red wine is spilled on a fabric, blot the area gently (don't rub, otherwise you'll set the stain). Next, pour cold water over the stain and cover the area with salt. The salt will start to turn pink as it absorbs the wine. At this point, you can either use a pre-treatment solution and throw it in the wash, or take the additional step of pouring boiling water over the fabric to release the stain. This is typically done by stretching the fabric over a bowl and pouring the water from a height above it.

SUCK OUT THE BLOOD

Salt can also help remove blood stains. Make a paste of salt and water, and rub it into the stain. An old toothbrush can make this task easier. Wash the garment as soon as possible.

Bonus tip: You can also soak a recently blood-stained item in salt water for a few hours before washing.

 ## BLOOD STAINS

For blood stains, sprinkle the area immediately with baking soda. If the fabric is colorfast, then rub in a little hydrogen peroxide to lift the stain. Wash the garment immediately.

 ## ARTIFICIAL-FLOWER CLEANER

Silk and artificial flowers can be tricky to clean. They gather a lot of dust and can absorb oils and dirt. To get them clean, try this ingenious tip. Place them in a bag with one half to three quarter cup salt, and shake well for a minute. Carefully remove the flowers, and shake off any excess salt. This approach is much easier than trying to clean or dust each petal by hand.

 IRON CLEANER

Starched shirts look prim and proper, but the starch itself can leave a toll on your iron. To remove the buildup, wipe down a cool, unplugged iron plate with vinegar until the residue is gone. Wipe again with a cloth lightly dampened in water and dry.

  ELIMINATE IRON SCORCH MARKS

If you've accidentally ironed a synthetic fabric at a too-hot temperature, then you know that fabric can sometimes "melt" a little bit and stick to the iron, leaving behind a mark on the soleplate. To remove it, when the iron is cool and unplugged, mix together a paste of baking soda and vinegar and rub the marks away. Be sure to remove any baking soda–vinegar residue from the plate with a damp cloth.

 OR TRY . . .

Place an old rag on the ironing board and sprinkle the surface generously with salt. Turn the iron on high and iron over the salt several times. The heat combined with the scouring power of the salt will remove whatever melted on the soleplate. Make sure the steam function is off when you do this; otherwise, the salt will start to dissolve, and you'll have a wet mess on your hands.

HOUSEHOLD HINTS

  RUST STAINS

Rust stains are very difficult to remove from fabric. Before giving up all hope, though, try the salt, lemon, and sun method listed in the previous tip. If you notice that the stains start to lighten, keep repeating the treatment. If you see no effect, then you might just have to live with the stain or try taking the garment to a professional.

 INK STAINS

Ink stains can also be very difficult to remove from fabric, but they are easier to treat than rust marks. Mix together equal parts lemon juice and liquid laundry detergent, then apply it to the stain. Let sit a few hours and launder as usual.

 HELP FOR THE HAMPER

The laundry hamper is a common spot for odors to accumulate. Keep it smelling fresh by sprinkling it regularly with baking soda.

 A SHOE-IN

Here's another classic tip: At night, sprinkle the insides of shoes with baking soda to help eliminate foot odors and perspiration. Simply dump or vacuum out the baking soda before wearing.

 A PICK-ME-UP FOR SUEDE

Since suede can't easily be cleaned, use baking soda to freshen it up. Sprinkle the item with baking soda, using a soft-bristled brush to evenly distribute. Let it sit for an hour or two to absorb oils and odors. Then simply brush away the baking soda (along with any other accumulated dust and dirt) and you'll be set.

Common Items

MAKE YOUR OWN YOGA MAT CLEANER

You may be trying to perfect your sirsasana, but if your yoga mat stinks you're probably not going to be able to focus on your breathing. Keep it clean the eco-friendly way with a homemade mat spray. In a spray bottle, mix one part vinegar, a drop or two of dish soap, and three parts water. Spray the mat liberally with the solution and wipe down with a cloth. Then rinse with plain water. Allow to dry completely before rolling up and storing.

GENTLE YOGA MAT CLEANER

For a gentle, deodorizing yoga mat cleaner, mix one part baking soda with four parts water. Wipe down the mat with the solution, then rinse by wiping down with a cloth dampened with just water. Allow the mat to dry.

FOR A CLEANER CELL PHONE

Your cell phone is a magnet for dirt and germs. To clean and disinfect it, mix together one tablespoon vinegar and one tablespoon water. When your phone is turned off, very lightly dampen a microfiber cloth with this mixture and use it to wipe down the screen and exterior. The key here is that you don't want to get the phone wet because liquids are like kryptonite to most electronic devices. The cloth should be barely damp, and you should avoid all openings. Buff with a dry cloth.

RAGS TO RICHES

If you're not already a fan of rags, consider becoming a convert. Rags can reduce or even eliminate your paper towel usage, saving both money and paper. Instead of tossing out old shirts, lone socks, and hole-filled fitted sheets, give them a new life as rags. Larger pieces of fabric can  be cut into more manageable sizes and stored in a nice basket or box in the closet. Use them to wipe down countertops, clean up spills, and more. Stick an old sock on your hand and dust blinds, banisters, and other tight spots. Dry the car by hand with an old T-shirt. The best part? Dirty rags can be washed and reused countless times.

Clever Household Tricks

 ## UNCLOG A TOILET

Clear a toilet clog with the fizzing power of baking soda and vinegar. First, bale out as much water as you can to prevent overflowing. Next, pour in one to two cups baking soda, then *very slowly* pour in an equal amount of vinegar, which will, of course, fizz on contact. Wait twenty to thirty minutes, then flush. If the clog still doesn't clear, pour very hot water into the toilet, wait a minute or two, then flush again.

 ## HOMEMADE AIR FRESHENERS

Remove the pulp from half a lemon and fill the cavity with salt, and place anywhere in your home that needs a little freshening. The salt will help eliminate odor and the lemon will provide a nice aroma.

 ## DIY POTPOURRI

Use dried lemon peels to make your own potpourri. In most climates, the peels will dry naturally at room temperature in a few days. If you'd like to speed up the process, you can try drying them on a baking sheet in a low oven (150–200°F). Check after one hour. If they need more time, continue to check every fifteen minutes or so until dry, but don't let them burn. Mix the cooled, dried peels with other sweet-smelling ingredients like cloves, cinnamon, star anise, dried apple slices, or whatever you prefer.

MAKE YOUR CANDLES DRIPLESS

Ever wonder how to stop candles from dripping on your tablecloth? A soak in very salty water should do it. This is a great tip if you've got some inexpensive candles on hand that you've been wanting to use, but are afraid they will drip all over your tablecloth. Soak them for anywhere from a few hours to a full twenty-four hours. Remove from the water and dry before storing or using.

 LONGER-LASTING FLOWERS

There's nothing quite like fresh flowers for a pick-me-up. Whether they're the pride of your garden or simply a bunch that caught your eye at the supermarket, make them last longer with vinegar and sugar. Place two tablespoons white vinegar and two tablespoons sugar in a vase, then fill with water. Cut the flower stems at a 45-degree angle so that they can take in the water, and place them in the vase. The vinegar helps slow down the development of bacteria, and the sugar feeds the blooms. For best results, change the water regularly.

 OR TRY . . .

Lemon juice can also help cut flowers last longer. Add two tablespoons lemon juice and one tablespoon sugar to the water, and insert the flowers.

WALLPAPER REMOVER

Need to remove wallpaper? In a spray bottle, mix together half white vinegar and half hot water. Spray the wallpaper that you'd like to remove, and allow the vinegar-water mix to saturate the surface for ten minutes or so before you start scraping. This tip should make removing the wallpaper a lot easier, but no one ever said the job was easy.

 ## NEW BROOM TIP

It's said that if you soak a new straw broom in potent, hot salt water before using it, it will last longer. Recommendations are for anywhere from twenty minutes to several hours.

 STICK TIGHT

Surprisingly enough, in addition *removing* wallpaper, vinegar can also help paint *stick* better. If you're painting a concrete or metal surface, wipe it down first with full-strength vinegar. After it's completely dry, paint as usual.

   **COIN TRICK**

Want to clean up some old corroded pennies? Put them in a bath of vinegar to which you've added about one teaspoon of salt. After about ten minutes, they'll look like new. (Kids love this trick.)
Try This Twist: You can also get the same effect by soaking the pennies in lemon juice for a few minutes. Whichever variation you use, rinse the pennies well in water and allow them to dry.

CHAPTER 2

FOOD AND COOKING

SALT, LEMON, VINEGAR, and baking soda are—first and foremost—everyday ingredients in the kitchen. Salt is in almost every food we consume, even sweet ones. Any baker worth his salt, so to speak, knows that cakes, pies, and cookies almost always include a small amount of salt; without it, they taste flat and bland. Salt is a preservative and essential for curing foods like prosciutto, jamón serrano, salami, smoked salmon, and others. Many chefs have said that if they were restricted to just one ingredient to season food, they'd have to choose salt. It is that magic element that enhances flavor in an irreplaceable way: ask anyone who's had to reduce or eliminate sodium from the diet because of high blood pressure or other health reasons. In recent years, more and more different kinds of salt have become popular on the American table—to the point that some people even hold salt tastings to understand the subtleties in flavor among the different varieties.

Vinegar is crucial to making a tasty salad dressing, of course, but it's also a key ingredient in marinades for vegetables, fish, and meat. It can cut the richness of sauces and add balance and brightness to foods both savory and sweet. Like salt, vinegar is used to preserve and store food, and the world's cuisine is rich with vinegar-based dishes. Think of Filipino chicken adobo, Latin American escabeches, and North Carolina barbecues. And we can pickle almost anything from cucumbers, green beans, and jalapeños to eggs, watermelon rinds, and plums. (Indeed, I couldn't resist sharing my own recipe for refrigerator pickles on page 142.) The sheer diversity of vinegars—including balsamic, sherry, rice wine, champagne, and countless others—multiplies their many uses.

Lemon can do many of the same things that vinegar can do, but its unique citric tang is a required ingredient in pies—imagine a blueberry pie without lemon juice and zest—and many baked goods. Added at the end of the cooking process, a squeeze of lemon brightens vegetables, cuts richness in meats, and adds a special something to sauces. A lemon wedge is almost mandatory on a plate of fish and many other dishes.

Middle Eastern cuisine, for example, relies heavily on the use of preserved lemons in various foods. (These lemons are conserved, coincidentally, in salt.)

Compared with salt, lemon, and vinegar, the uses of the leavening agent baking soda seem more limited. But without it cakes, cookies, quick breads, pancakes, and other baked goods would fall flat. In addition, baking soda can be used to balance the acidity in too-tart foods.

While this is not a cookbook, it would be remiss to overlook the many "aha" uses of our four magical ingredients for food and cooking. This chapter collects dozens of these uses from the familiar—such as adding lemon to keep fruit salad from browning—to the surprising, such as using salt to cool down a bottle of wine in a jiffy.

FOOD

Fish

 SAY NO TO FUNKY FISH SMELLS

Fresh fish is a healthy and delicious dinner option, but if you're the one preparing it, you might not like the odor the raw fish leaves on your hands. To remove it, just dip your fingertips in a little bit of lemon juice or vinegar. (Skip this tip if you have cuts or broken skin, as the acidic lemon juice or vinegar will sting.)

FOR FRESHER-TASTING FISH

A vinegar- or citrus-based marinade will help remove the fishy flavor from fish. Note that if you let the fish marinate too long, the vinegar (or juice) will start to "cook" the fish (see the ceviche tip below). Keep marinating times to thirty to sixty minutes for most fillets, then grill, sauté, or bake as your recipe directs.

Traditional to Latin America, ceviche is a dish made from raw fish cured in lemon or lime juice. The fish is cut in bite-sized pieces and tossed with other ingredients like onions, hot peppers, tomatoes, and cilantro. About a one half cup of lemon or lime juice per pound of fish is added to create the marinade. The fish is then refrigerated for anywhere between fifteen minutes and a few hours, and when it's ready, the citrus juice will have given the fish the appearance of being cooked. Food-borne illness is, however, still a risk; for that reason, only the freshest fish are selected. If you'd like to try ceviche, but are a little wary about the raw fish aspect, why not try substituting cooked seafood like shrimp, octopus, and squid? Decrease the marinating time, then serve. It will still be delicious.

 ## ON THE SIDE

It's no surprise that fish is often served with a wedge of lemon. The kick of acidity highlights the fish's delicate flavor and is suitable for almost every recipe.

 ## SEAFOOD SURPRISE

For a dramatic dinner party presentation, consider a recipe for a salt-encrusted whole fish. This is a great idea when you want the flavor of an ultra-fresh fish to shine. The fish's cavity is stuffed with herbs and seasonings, and then the whole fish is covered in a crust of *several cups* (no, that's not a typo) of salt mixed together with egg whites and a bit of water. While the fish is in the oven it steams in the salt crust and stays incredibly moist, and most surprising of all, doesn't get too salty. The crust is cracked open with a flourish, removed, and then discarded.

FAVORITE HOME REMEDIES: LEMON

Lemons are one of the most versatile and well-known home remedies. Still, it's a good idea to check with your doctor, especially if you're taking medication or suffer from any condition.

Drink lemon-and-honey tea for a cold. Almost as good as chicken soup, lemon-and-honey tea should be your go-to home remedy for a cold. The astringent lemon burns (in a good way) a sore throat and the sweet honey soothes it. The hot steam also helps to loosen congestion. What's not to love? Squeeze a half or whole lemon in a cup of hot water and add honey to taste. **Try This Twist:** Add fresh ginger for extra immune-system benefits.

DIY cough syrup. Mix together lemon juice and honey and take this as a simple cough syrup for a mild cough.

Freshen breath with lemon. Add a squeeze of lemon to your water to keep your breath smelling sweet.

Regulate your digestion. If you've been suffering from constipation, lemon water might help get you back on track. Before breakfast, drink a glass of water to which you've added several tablespoons of lemon juice. If it's too sour for your taste, add a spoonful of honey. The lemon water can help stimulate the colon.

Treat a minor cut. In a pinch, you can wash out a minor cut with a squeeze of lemon juice, but it will sting on contact.

Help with hiccups. There are a 1,001 hiccup remedies, and here's one of them: suck on a wedge of lemon to stop the hiccups.

Drinks

 ## SUPER-SPEEDY WINE COOLER

Every once in a while, you've got something to celebrate—stat! Chill a bottle of wine in a flash with a secret weapon: salt. Fill a large pot or ice bucket with ice and a few big handfuls of salt. Add water, and mix so that the salt is evenly distributed. Stick the bottle of wine in the bucket, and wait ten minutes. Your wine will be cold and ready to serve. You'll never dread surprise houseguests again.

Try This Twist: At your next picnic, add salt to ice in a cooler filled with beer and soda for extra-cold refreshments.

 ## ONE TEQUILA, TWO TEQUILA . . .

Salt and lime soften the harshness of a tequila shot. The salt is traditionally licked from the side of your hand before downing the tequila. Bite down on a lime wedge to finish.

 ## CLASSIC MARGARITA TIP

For a perfectly balanced margarita, be sure to add salt to the rim. To help the salt adhere, first dampen the rim of the glass with water, then dip it in salt.

 A (LESS) BITTER PILL TO SWALLOW

Whether you just don't like the dark French roast your aunt gave you for Christmas, or you simply added too much coffee to the brew basket, there's a simple way to reduce coffee's bitterness: a pinch of salt. A small pinch per pot will offset the unpleasant flavor, making your morning java a little tastier. Don't overdo it, or you'll just have salty coffee.

 LESSEN COFFEE'S ACIDITY

Some people find that the acidity in coffee causes stomach irritation. To reduce coffee's bite, add a pinch of baking soda to your cup. If you're skeptical, remember that baking soda is often used to treat heartburn.

THE SECRET TO SWEET TEA

When making a Southern-style sweet iced tea, add a pinch of baking soda to the pitcher to smooth over any bitterness in the tannins and make the tea darker.

 ## BEVERAGE BOOSTER

A wedge of lemon can perk up most drinks: try it in cola, seltzer, tap water, iced tea, and more.

 ## A LEMON LIFT FOR ESPRESSO

A thin slice of lemon peel is often served with espresso. Just twist it to release the natural oils, and rub it over the rim of the cup before drinking.

Substitutions

 ## HOW TO HONEY SWAP

Want to substitute honey for sugar in a baking recipe? Baking soda is the magic ingredient you'll need in order to successfully make the switch. For each cup of sugar you want to replace, substitute about three quarters of a cup honey and one quarter to one half teaspoon baking soda. The alkalinity in the baking soda offsets the slightly acidic honey. Reduce the oven temperature by 25°F because baked goods made with honey brown more quickly.

 ## BAKING POWDER SUBSTITUTE

If the cake recipe you want to make calls for baking *powder*, and you only have baking *soda* on hand at the moment, check your pantry. If you've also got cream of tartar and cornstarch, you'll be able to save yourself a trip to the store. For each teaspoon of baking powder the recipe calls for, sift together one half teaspoon cream of tartar, one quarter teaspoon baking soda, and one quarter teaspoon cornstarch. Add to your batter and bake as soon as possible for best results.

Good to Know: Don't mix up more than you need because this substitution doesn't store as well as a commercial double-acting baking powder.

BUTTERMILK SUBSTITUTE

You were planning on making buttermilk pancakes for breakfast, but there's just one problem: you forgot to buy the buttermilk. Don't worry because the substitute is both easy and extremely effective. To replace one cup of buttermilk, place one tablespoon white vinegar, apple cider vinegar, or lemon juice in a glass measuring cup, then add milk to reach the one cup mark. Stir and wait ten minutes. During this time, the milk will start to curdle, creating what is called "clabbered milk." Simply add the curdled milk to the recipe and proceed.

FIRE STOPPER

Baking soda can help put out a small grease fire in a pan, but you'll need to use a large quantity. You should also turn off the heat immediately. If you can do it safely, cover the pan with a non-glass lid to smother the fire (a glass lid could shatter). And never use water on a grease fire.

Try This Twist: If you don't have any baking soda nearby, a large amount of salt can also be used to smother a small fire.

 ## SAVE YOUR SALSA

For homemade salsas and guacamole, fresh lime juice is the key ingredient needed to give tang and brightness to those condiments—as well as to pull all of these disparate ingredients like onion, garlic, cilantro, and jalapeño together. But if you open your crisper drawer and see you're out of lime, you can substitute apple cider or white vinegar in a pinch.

  ## ONE FOR THE OTHER

In most instances, unless a particular flavor is needed, if you're out of either lemon or vinegar, you can substitute one for the other.

  ## EGG SUBSTITUTE

Your cake recipe calls for three eggs, but you just realized you only have two—and you're already too far into the recipe to stop and head to the store. Replace the missing egg with one teaspoon baking soda and one tablespoon of white vinegar. It will provide the missing lift that the egg would have provided. Some substitution guides also suggest the addition of a teaspoon or two of water with the baking soda and vinegar.

Eggs

 FOR FLUFFY SCRAMBLED EGGS

If you like fluffy scrambled eggs, you'll love this tip. Add a pinch of baking soda or baking powder per egg to the bowl while you beat the eggs, and you'll end up with delicate, delicious eggs.

 HOW TO FREEZE EGG YOLKS

Did an angel food cake recipe leave you with lots of spare egg yolks and nothing to do with them? Don't toss them—freeze them. For every four yolks, beat in one eighth teaspoon salt. Portion them off into containers or bags and then freeze. For best results, use within a year of freezing. Egg yolks are good for spaghetti carbonara, crème brûlée, hollandaise sauce, and many other possibilities.

 EGG PEELING MADE EASY

When hard-boiling eggs, add a teaspoon or two of vinegar to the water to make the eggs easier to peel. After they're done, plunge them in an ice-water bath until cool enough to handle.

POACHING TO PERFECTION

Here's a classic tip for poached eggs: add a splash of vinegar and a pinch of salt to the cooking water to help the whites set up more quickly. The eggs will also be easier to handle.

  ## EGG-CELLENT EGGS

Want silky smooth scrambled eggs? For every two eggs, add one and a half teaspoons vinegar or lemon juice when you beat them. Or, for a twist, drizzle the eggs with a few drops of sherry vinegar, rice wine vinegar, or balsamic vinegar at the end. Top with a nice pinch of flaky Maldon salt or fleur de sel.

9 CLEVER KITCHEN USES FOR COOKING OILS

Olive oil is great for salads, flavoring foods, and heart-healthy cooking. Canola and other vegetable oils can be used for high-heat cooking or whenever a neutral-flavored oil is needed. The latest trendsetter, coconut oil, can be used for everything from a spread on toast and a stir-fry oil to a replacement for your moisturizer. Let's explore some more of the best kitchen tips for cooking oils.

1. **Raise butter's smoke point—and use less of it.** If you're sautéing vegetables or meat in butter, you can stop the butter from browning too quickly by adding a little bit of oil. It will allow you to cook at a higher heat, and you'll still get the delicious butter flavor. However, if you wish to cut the saturated fat, just replace half or even all of the butter with olive oil.

2. **Measure sticky substances with ease.** Your recipe calls for one quarter cup of honey, but when you pour it into your mixing bowl about one third of it stays behind in the measuring cup. Make it slide out easily by greasing the cup with a bit of oil. It will also make cleanup a breeze.

3. **Bread and (not) butter.** You've probably seen this in restaurants: dip your daily bread in a high-quality extra-virgin olive oil instead of spreading it with butter.

4. **Do a dairy-free frosting.** Whether by choice or for health reasons, you may not want to add that stick of or two of butter to your cake frosting recipe. Swap in coconut oil instead. Just make sure the coconut oil is solid at room temperature where you live (in warmer climates, it's a liquid); if not, refrigerate it until it is. You might also want to store the finished item in the fridge to make sure it keeps the right consistency.

5. **Season a cast-iron skillet. . .** Whether you've just bought a new cast-iron pan or you've revived an old, rusty one, you'll need to give it a good seasoning before using it. (This will create a nonstick-like finish without the chemicals found in nonstick pans.) Coat a clean, dry pan with a thin layer of vegetable oil and place it on a baking sheet or layer of aluminum foil in a 350°F oven for one hour. Allow it to cool completely in the oven before removing.

6. **. . . And keep it seasoned.** Once you've got your cast-iron pan seasoned, make sure you maintain it. After washing it, put a little oil on a paper towel or rag and rub it all over the pan before storing it.

7. **Make foods pop.** A little drizzle of a top-quality extra-virgin olive oil on tonight's dinner can transform a good meal into a great one.

8. **Keep pasta from sticking.** As soon as you drain cooked pasta into a colander, it seems bent on gluing itself into a solid mass. Dump it back into the pan and toss it quickly with a little olive oil to keep the strands separate.

9. **Make healthier popcorn.** Instead of drowning popcorn in melted butter, use coconut oil instead. For a vegan treat, sprinkle with seasoned nutritional yeast.

Potatoes

 MAGNIFICENT MASHED POTATOES

For delicious mashed potatoes, add buttermilk and a pinch of baking soda. The baking soda will make them lighter and fluffier and the buttermilk will give a wonderful tangy flavor.

  POTATO PREP

Here's a great tip for Thanksgiving when you're trying to get as much of the cooking done ahead of time as possible. Keep peeled potatoes from turning brown by putting them in water to cover and adding a splash of vinegar or lemon juice. Keep them in the refrigerator until you're ready to proceed with your recipe.

Fresh Test: To test and see if your baking soda is still fresh, pour a little bit into a bowl and start adding either lemon juice or vinegar. If it fizzes strongly, then it's still fresh. If not, relegate that box to other uses like cleaning or deodorizing the drain, and open a fresh box for baking and cooking.

 CHIP SHOP

To enjoy your fries—er, "chips"—British-style, sprinkle them with malt vinegar.

Desserts

 A MUST FOR CARAMEL CORN

When making caramel for caramel corn, stir in one half teaspoon baking soda at the end to keep the caramel soft and pliable.

 SALTY-SWEET PERFECTION

You've probably tried or at least heard of the wildly popular salted caramel by now. The salty-sweet combination is a modern classic, but you can also try a sprinkle of Maldon salt or fleur de sel on ice cream, cookies, cakes, pies, and more.

 GO FLAKY

Bakers know that the secret ingredient for a tender, flaky piecrust is vinegar. One to two teaspoons of apple cider or white vinegar is all you need.

A SATISFYING STRAWBERRY DESSERT

Strawberries and balsamic vinegar are perfect partners, and together they make a very popular dessert. This is one time where you want a very high quality balsamic vinegar: think those expensive little bottles in the gourmet market, not your regular supermarket brand. Drizzle a bowl of cut strawberries with a little bit of vinegar and about the same amount of sugar. Toss lightly. Let sit for ten minutes or so to allow the flavors to meld, adjust seasonings as needed, then serve immediately.

Try This Twist: To sweeten up the balsamic vinegar even more, reduce it in a saucepan until it's nice and syrupy. You can even put it on ice cream.

THE DIFFERENCE BETWEEN BAKING POWDER AND BAKING SODA

If a recipe calls for baking powder or baking soda, can you just substitute one for the other? The short answer is no, but both *are* leaveners. Baking soda, an alkaline, needs to interact with an acid like lemon juice or buttermilk to work. (Think of the fizzing action when vinegar hits baking soda, for example.) This chemical reaction provides lift. Baking powder, on the other  hand, contains about one third baking soda, but it also contains ingredients like cornstarch and cream of tartar that interact with moisture and heat to rise. If you run out of baking powder, see the substitute on page 127.

Meats

MEAT TENDERIZER

To tenderize beef or pork for a stir-fry, cut it into bite-sized pieces and toss in a bowl with one teaspoon baking soda per pound. Refrigerate the meat for twenty to thirty minutes, then rinse and dry it before proceeding with your recipe.

BASIC MEAT MARINADE

Vinegar is an inexpensive and terrific choice for tenderizing and marinating meat. You can use plain white, apple cider, or even a nice sherry or red wine vinegar. Add in other ingredients like salt, pepper, your favorite herbs and spices, and little bit of olive oil. Refrigerate the meat for several hours or even overnight before cooking.

SALT SPLURGE

For an elegant touch when serving a nice steak or lamb, pass a fancy salt like Maldon or fleur de sel at the table. Just a few flakes sprinkled on top of the meat add a fabulous burst of flavor and contrast of texture. If you're concerned about your sodium intake, go light on the amount of salt you add to the meat before cooking.

Good to Know: Many people rinse meat with vinegar as a way of cleaning it before cooking. While this may add flavor to a recipe, it's not generally recommended as a cleaning practice because of the possibility of spreading germs from the raw meat onto other surfaces. The USDA warns that consumers should not wash meat, particularly chicken, because of the risk of cross-contamination; plus, and most importantly, the kinds of germs that could make you sick can only be killed by cooking.

Fruits and Vegetables

 BAKING SODA FOR BEANS?

Some believe that adding a pinch of baking soda to the soaking liquid for beans will reduce the gaseous effects that beans can have on some people. Whether accurate or not, however, some experts have found that the baking soda can leach out some of the vital nutrients in the beans, particularly thiamine, so if you use this method, be sure to rinse the beans before boiling.

 COOK'S TIP

While it's often said that cooking dried beans in salted water will cause them to toughen and cook unevenly, the same is apparently not true for soaking them. Test cooks at the venerable *Cook's Illustrated* magazine found that if you dissolve three tablespoons salt in one gallon of water, and use this brine to soak one pound of beans, you'll get much softer skins. Just be sure to drain and rinse the beans before cooking.

BAN BROWN FRUIT

Keep your fruit salad fresher longer by tossing it with a tablespoon of lemon juice. It will keep it from turning brown, a must if the salad includes fruits like bananas, apples, and pears. Plus, the lemon gives it a lovely flavor.

 ## PRESERVE THE COLOR OF CABBAGE

Red cabbage tends to lose its color when cooked. In order to preserve it, add a bit of vinegar to the saucepan.

 ## SAUTÉING SUGGESTION

If a recipe calls for you to sauté vegetables like onions, carrots, and peppers without browning, add a pinch of salt to the skillet. Salt helps the vegetables release water, so they'll soften, not caramelize and brown.

 ## HOW TO STORE AN AVOCADO

Leftover avocado browns quickly, but you can help make it last longer by sprinkling it with lemon juice and covering it tightly with plastic wrap. It's also said that storing the avocado with the pit in place will preserve it.

 ## LEMON JUICING TIP

To get the maximum amount of juice from your lemon, try rolling it on the counter while pressing firmly on it; this breaks some of the segments making the juice easier to squeeze when you cut the lemon open. You can also microwave a lemon for twenty seconds before juicing it.

 ## REAMER REPLACER

Don't have a lemon reamer? A fork can work just as well.

 ## SECRET WATERMELON "SWEETENER"

Some people add a pinch of salt to watermelon before eating it. They say it makes it taste sweeter.

 ## LEMON AID

Don't waste any part of the lemon. Use a zester or Microplane to remove the zest even if it you don't have an immediate use for it. It will keep well in the freezer for several months. Lemon zest can be added to recipes for cakes, muffins, cookies, soups, stews, vegetables, sorbets, and more.

GARLIC-DILL REFRIGERATOR PICKLES

I love a good, crispy, deli-style dill pickle, but I can't often find them where I live, hence this recipe for refrigerator pickles. They have the crunch and tanginess I'm looking for, and they're also super-easy. The best part is that you don't need to fuss with canning equipment: just stick them in the fridge. They taste even better a few days after they're made, and they'll last several weeks—if they don't get eaten up much sooner. In-season pickling cucumbers, like kirbys, are your best bet, but I often grab a bag of tender baby cucumbers from our local ware-house store. I'm firmly in the sour (never sweet-and-sour) pickle camp. This recipe includes garlic, but you can leave it out. Other possible add-ins include sliced onions, peppercorns, crushed red pepper, sliced jala-peños, carrots, and bell peppers.

1½–2 pounds pickling or baby cucumbers, left whole or cut into spears

2–3 sprigs fresh dill (left whole)

4 large garlic cloves, crushed

1½ cups white or apple cider vinegar

1½ cups water

1 tablespoon kosher salt, plus more to taste

1. Place the cucumbers in a container large enough to hold both them and the pickling liquid. (I use a rectangular Tupperware-style container.) Add in the dill and garlic, if using.

2. In a medium saucepan, bring the vinegar, water, and salt to a boil. After it's come to a boil, you'll want to check the salt levels and add additional salt, if needed, to taste. (Careful: the mixture is hot!) If you find the mixture too vinegary, you can also add in a little extra water.

3. Remove the brine from the heat and allow to cool for a few minutes before pouring over the pickles. When the pickles have reached room temperature, cover them and refrigerate. (Resist the temptation to try them for at least 24 hours, so they have a chance to absorb the pickling liquid.)

BAKING-SODA WASH FOR PRODUCE

Instead of using a food spray, clean fruits and vegetables with baking soda. Dissolve a few tablespoons in a basin of water and use it to scrub or rinse produce before consuming. Follow this up with a rinse in plain water and allow the fruit or vegetables to dry on a towel.

 ## OR TRY . . .

You can use a vinegar and water solution to clean fruits and vegetables. Mix together one part vinegar and three parts water in a spray bottle, and spray to coat. Rinse well with water, so that there's no lingering vinegar flavor. The vinegar helps cut down on the number of bacteria on the outside of the food.

 ## OR TRY . . .

Need to wash lettuce or other greens? Separate the leaves, and soak them in a basin filled with water and one cup vinegar. Rinse well and dry on a towel or in a salad spinner.

 ## A NEW LIFE FOR LIMP LETTUCE

Before tossing out that slightly wilted lettuce in your crisper drawer, see if you can perk it back up with some lemon water. Squeeze half a lemon in a bowl of cold water and soak the lettuce for thirty minutes in the refrigerator.

 ## LEMON DRESSING

For a break from vinegar-based salad dressings, substitute lemon in your vinaigrette. Add minced shallots and Dijon mustard for a French twist.

 ## BERRY-STAIN REMOVER

Blueberries are notorious for staining everything they come in contact with, including your fingers. To remove the stain, scrub your fingers in vinegar.

 ## OR TRY . . .

Rub away berry stains with lemon juice.

SEED SPROUTING

Alfalfa, mung bean, lentil, and other sprouts can be fun to grow at home. But you've likely also heard of the food-safety concerns with sprouts: some seeds, even organic ones, can harbor *E. coli* and *salmonella* bacteria inside them, and these bacteria can multiply rapidly during the sprouting process. However, according to the University of California, you can make sprouting safer with regular 3% hydrogen peroxide. In a small saucepan heated to 140°F, stir the seeds for five minutes, then drain and rinse well for one minute.[15] Remove any floating seeds or seed fragments, and be sure to use seeds specifically marked for sprouting.

KITCHEN HACKS

 ## SWEETEN A SAUCE

If your big, simmering pot of marinara has a little too much acidic bite to it, you can soften it with baking soda. It will increase the alkalinity in the sauce, so that it tastes a little sweeter. Start with one quarter teaspoon and go from there. Other alternatives include a pinch of sugar and a pat of butter.

 ## TOO MUCH SALT?

Heavy hand on the salt? Add one half teaspoon of vinegar to the dish, and taste it again. Continue adding vinegar in one half teaspoon increments until the salty flavor is lessened.

 ## SMOOTH FONDUE

You may only take out the fondue pot once a year, but when you do, don't forget the baking soda. A pinch added at the end along with the kirsch will make for a lighter and smoother cheese sauce.

 ## SOFTEN A SOUR DISH

For a dish that's turned out too sour or vinegary, add a pinch of baking soda to tame the acidity and save dinner.

 ## FOR FREE-FLOWING SALT

This tip has been spotted in virtually every diner in America: add a few grains of rice to a salt shaker to avoid clumps and keep the salt flowing freely.

CHEESE SAVER

You just couldn't resist buying a huge block of cheddar on super-sale at the warehouse store, but you're not quite sure how your family will eat it all before it goes bad. Wrap the cheese in a paper towel soaked in vinegar; the vinegar will inhibit mold growth and make the cheese last longer. You can also rinse the cheese with vinegar before storing.

Try This Twist: Instead of vinegar, soak a paper towel in salt water and wrap the cheese with it to prevent mold.

 ## FLAVOR BURST

A flat-tasting soup or stew can be brightened up by adding vinegar. A teaspoon of your favorite vinegar could be just the acidic boost you need to make the dish come together.

CHAPTER 3

GARDEN, GARAGE, YARD, PETS, AND PESTS

WHILE THERE MAY not be as many outdoor uses for salt, lemon, vinegar, and baking soda as there are indoor uses, you'll still find quite a few in this chapter. Tackle the pool area with baking soda and vinegar. Keep your backyard barbecue-ready with a clean grill, sparkling patio furniture, and a lush lawn. Organic gardeners can use salt, lemon, vinegar, and baking soda in the garden to control pests and plant diseases and improve crop production. Don't neglect the car and garage either. Baking soda can freshen the interior, vinegar or lemon can polish chrome, and salt can clean up oil stains. Finally, at the end of the chapter, we'll explore how you can use these four ingredients to battle common pests, like ants and roaches. We'll even look at how your pet can benefit.

POOL

 BALANCE PH LEVELS

Baking soda can help balance the pH of your swimming pool. If you need to raise alkalinity, you can add several pounds of baking soda to bring it to the correct levels. The exact amount needed depends on the number of gallons in your pool and the pH level you need to reach. Arm & Hammer offers an online guide to baking soda usage in the pool at http://www.armandhammer.com/PDF/APoolOwnersGuide.pdf. In addition, large bags of baking soda will offer instructions on quantity.

 CLEAN THE KIDDIE POOL

If you have an inflatable or hard plastic pool for the kids, you can clean it with baking soda. Just sprinkle the surface with baking soda, add a little bit of warm water and scrub with a non-abrasive sponge. Use a hose to rinse and allow to dry completely in the sun.

 KEEP POOL TOYS CLEAN

Inner tubes, inflatable sea creatures, rafts, and more—pool toys can be a blast, and they are also super-easy to keep clean. Just dissolve one half cup baking soda in a gallon of warm water and wipe the toys with a damp rag. Rinse well with water and allow to dry before storing.

 NO ANTS IN THE POOL

To keep ants out of the pool area, spray the perimeter of the pool—or wherever you see them gather—with a mix of half vinegar, half water.

PATIO & GRILL

 OUTDOOR FURNITURE MAINTENANCE

Keep your patio furniture looking sharp with baking soda. Dissolve one half cup baking soda in a gallon of warm water and use it to clean the furniture. Rinse with a hose and allow to dry in the sun. For stains, apply a paste of baking soda and water and scrub until removed.

 BRIGHTER WICKER

Wicker furniture can be cleaned and brightened with salt water. Allow to dry in the sun.

GO-TO GRILL CLEANER

Everyone loves the food that comes off your grill in the summertime, but no one seems to want to clean up the mess for you. Baking soda can help tackle the job. Move the dirty grate to a surface that's large enough for you to work on. A large sink is a good idea, but if the grate is too big, then take it outside and place it on a plastic garbage bag. Sprinkle the entire grate with baking soda. Using a damp grill brush and spraying with water as needed, brush the grate until it's clean. Rinse with warm water.

Try This Twist: If you need to boost the abrasive action, mix some salt in with the baking soda.

 ## OR TRY . . .

If you're not getting much traction with the above method, you can try spraying vinegar on top of the baking soda. Allow the mixture to sit for a few hours to work on the burned food and grease, then scrub.

 ## OR TRY . . .

Generously spray the interior of a dirty grill with a mixture of half vinegar and half water. Wait an hour or two, then scrub clean with a grill brush.

FAVORITE HOME REMEDIES: SALT

I could probably dedicate a whole chapter to the home-remedy uses of salt, some time-tested and others more in the line of folk wisdom. Instead, I've narrowed down the field to some of the best and most effective. Still, it's a good idea to check with your doctor, especially if you're taking medication or suffer from any condition.

Soothe a sore throat with saltwater. Mom was right. And the Mayo Clinic agrees with her: a saltwater gargle can reduce the pain of a sore throat. Mix one half teaspoon salt in a cup of warm water and gargle for twenty seconds or so, then spit. The salt can reduce inflammation and loosen phlegm.

Calm a canker or cold sore. Just as for a sore throat, a saltwater rinse can help with canker or cold sores. Rinse with a quarter teaspoon salt dissolved in a cup of water.

Heal mouth wounds. If you have a tooth removed or other dental work done, your dentist may recommend saltwater rinses to keep the wound clean and as a general mouthwash.

Relax aching muscles with Epsom salt. Whether your muscles are sore from overuse or tense from stress, a bath of Epsom salt will help. The high concentration of magnesium is what relieves the pain along with the muscle-relaxing effect of the warm water. Add a full two cups to running bath water, and soak for about fifteen minutes.

Clean cuts and scrapes. Minor cuts and scrapes can be cleaned with a mild salt and water solution before dressing the wound.

Treat stings, splinters, and sunburn. A soak in Epsom salt can help soothe the pain of a sting, make a splinter easier to remove, *and* even alleviate the pain of a sunburn. How's that for versatility?

TOOL SHED

  RUSTY TOOL REMEDY

Don't let rusty tools get you down. Mix together salt with enough lemon juice to make a paste. Apply with a sponge or old toothbrush, and scrub until the rust disappears. Rinse to remove the paste and dry well.

 PAINTBRUSH SOFTENER AND CLEANER

Your Saturday painting project has been put on hold because you didn't exactly do a top-notch job cleaning your brushes last time around, and now they're hard as a rock. Not to worry—it's only a minor setback. Soak the brushes in hot vinegar for half an hour, which should loosen up the bristles enough so that you can remove the dried paint with a comb or brush. Finish by washing them thoroughly in hot, soapy water to remove any remaining residue.
Try This Twist: If you happen to have a lot of lemons or lemon juice on hand, you can substitute lemon juice for the vinegar, but given the quantity that you'd likely need, vinegar is a more budget-friendly solution.

 NAIL AND SCREW SAVER

Do you have a jar of rusty screws, nails, and washers? Instead of just tossing them in the trash, try soaking them overnight in vinegar. It can help remove the rust, so you might not need to buy replacements after all. Try a few first as an experiment to see if it will work for you. If you see progress after twenty-four hours, but the rust is not entirely gone, you may need to let them soak longer.

LAWN & GARDEN

 ## EPSOM SALTS TO FERTILIZE THE LAWN

Looking for a lush, green lawn? Epsom salts can be used as a fertilizer to boost your lawn's health, especially in areas with magnesium-deficient soil. You can use one tablespoon per gallon of water. A pump sprayer will help facilitate the process.

 ## OUTDOOR ANT PROBLEMS

Various methods abound for getting rid of anthills, including boiling water and diatomaceous earth. Vinegar works well too: pour it into the anthill and it will kill the ants on contact.

Try This Twist: Others swear by a combo of baking soda and vinegar: first sprinkle the anthill with baking soda and then pour on the vinegar.

 ## FOR THE BIRDS

A birdbath needs cleaning too. Scrub yours with a stiff brush and a mixture of half white or apple cider vinegar and half water. It will help disinfect the bath as well as remove algae, debris, and other residue. Rinse thoroughly with water to make sure that the vinegar solution is gone, then refill with clean water for the birds.

MORE NATURAL-GARDENING TIPS

HOMEMADE INSECTICIDAL SOAP

Don't want to spend money on an expensive insecticidal soap? Use dish soap. Mix together one tablespoon dishwashing liquid with four cups water, and use the soapy mixture to wash away scale, mealybugs, or other plant pests.

COFFEE TO COMPOST

Used coffee grounds are an excellent source of nitrogen for your compost pile. If you're not a coffee drinker, stop by your local café and ask if they can provide you with a free bag of grounds.

HYDROGEN PEROXIDE FOR FUNGUS

Hydrogen peroxide can help fight fungus in houseplants. Place two tablespoons hydrogen peroxide in a spray bottle filled with water, and mist the leaves of the plant every day until the fungus disappears.

POT CLEANER

If you use terracotta pots for container gardening, you know that over time they develop a whitish cast, thanks to a buildup of salts and other minerals. Many people like this rustic look; in fact, you'll even find online tutorials for creating it on brand-new pots. If, however, you'd prefer your pots look a bit more pristine, you can soak them in a solution of one part vinegar to four parts water. Use a firm-bristled brush to help remove the stains. Then rinse the pots in water and allow to dry before using. If the stains are really stubborn, increase the amount of vinegar.

TOMATO AND PEPPER BOOSTER

Want to grow more and better tomatoes and peppers? If your soil is magnesium-deficient, you can boost production with Epsom salt. When you transplant your seedlings into the garden, add one to two tablespoons of Epsom salt per hole.

HOUSEPLANT HELPER

Houseplants can benefit from Epsom salt as well. Dissolve one to two tablespoons in one gallon of water, and use to water your plants once or twice a month. It can help boost plant growth.

SHOW YOUR ROSES SOME LOVE

If you love roses, Epsom salt can help make your plants healthier and even boost flower production. Sprinkle a half cup or so around the base of the plant at the beginning of the season. You can also use Epsom salt as a spray for the leaves. Dissolve one tablespoon in one gallon of water.

 HELP FOR A SLUG PROBLEM

If slugs are feasting on the tender plants in your garden, leaving you wondering how much of what you sow you'll actually get to harvest, pay attention to this tip. Epsom salt is thought to help deter slugs, so sprinkle a little bit on the soil where you tend to see them. As an added benefit, the Epsom salt can improve your soil if it's magnesium deficient.

Good to Know: Regular salt can also kill slugs because the salt draws the water out of their body, but it's not advisable to use it in the garden because it is detrimental to plants.

  THE BAKING SODA AND VINEGAR SOIL TEST

You can buy commercial soil testing kits or even ship off a sample to your local extension service, but if you just need to know if your soil is acidic or alkaline, there's a quick and easy way to do it: with baking soda and vinegar. All you'll need to perform the test are two containers, a box of baking soda, a bottle of vinegar, and a little water. Place the soil you want to test in one container, and pour some vinegar over it. (You may want to stir it a bit to make sure the vinegar is evenly distributed.) If it fizzes, the soil is alkaline, meaning the pH is above 7. To test for acidity, in the other container, mix together the soil and water until muddy, then stir in some baking soda. If it fizzes, it's acidic, and the pH is below 7. If neither baking soda nor vinegar makes the soil fizz, your pH is neutral. By knowing this information, you can select plants that like either acidic or alkaline conditions, or you can take steps to improve the soil.

BAKING SODA FUNGICIDE

For an all-purpose natural fungicide, in one gallon of water, mix together one table-spoon baking soda, one teaspoon castile soap, and one tablespoon either vegetable oil (good) or horticultural oil (even better). Make sure that ingredients are thoroughly combined. Spray on diseased plants, being sure to remove dead leaves first, or use on healthy plants to prevent disease.

 BLACK SPOT FUNGUS FIGHTER

A simple mixture of baking soda and water can help prevent and fight black spot fungus, which attacks rose bushes and other plants. Two to three tablespoons baking soda per gallon of water is what you need; you can also add a little bit of horticultural soap to the mix if you'd like. Spray weekly for best results.

 LOOK, MA, CLEAN HANDS!

After an afternoon in the garden, you can clean your hands with baking soda. Use an old toothbrush or nail brush to dislodge dirt that's under your fingernails.

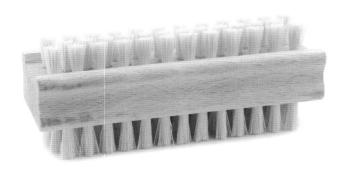

FAVORITE HOME REMEDIES: VINEGAR

These vinegar remedies range from tried-and-true to pretty modern, but either way many people swear by them. Even so, it's always a good idea to check with your doctor before using, especially if you're taking medication or suffer from any condition.

Soothe sunburn. While most people probably prefer the neutral-smelling aloe, it turns out that white vinegar can also tame the pain of sunburn. Just sponge it onto the skin for relief. Fortunately, the smell diminishes when it dries.

Prevent swimmer's ear. Swimmer's ear is an infection of the outer ear canal, and some swimmers are much more prone to it than others. To help keep swimmer's ear from taking hold, mix together a solution of one part white vinegar and one part rubbing alcohol and store the solution in a sterile bottle with an eye dropper. After swimming place a few drops in each ear canal. The vinegar helps to kill bacteria, and the alcohol helps to dry the ear canal quickly. Even the Centers for Disease Control and Prevention (CDC) has suggested this remedy, though they recommend getting the go-ahead from your doctor first—always a wise move.

Fight foot odor and treat foot conditions. Soak smelly feet in a foot basin to which you've added warm water and one cup white vinegar. This is a good tip for the summertime when your feet are more likely to be damp with perspiration. Be sure to rinse and dry them thoroughly. It's also said that daily vinegar soaks can help with nail fungus and athlete's foot because of vinegar's antifungal properties.

Lessen the pain of stings and insect bites. For an insect sting or bite, soak a cotton ball in a little bit of white vinegar and hold it on the area. It should relieve some of the pain and itchiness.

Control blood sugar. Some studies have shown a relationship between apple cider vinegar and blood sugar. It may control spikes in blood pressure, but it's no substitute for proper diet and medication.

Promote healthy digestion. Apple cider vinegar, particularly the kind you find in health-food stores that advertises all kinds of health benefits, may improve digestion. It contains healthy probiotics and may even make you more regular. Drink it in diluted form—about one tablespoon in a glass of water. And brush your teeth afterwards because vinegar can eat away at tooth enamel.

SIDEWALKS AND DRIVEWAY

 ## ROCK SALT SUBSTITUTE

While you almost certainly know that salt (in various formulations) is used to melt ice on surfaces like roads, driveways, and sidewalks, you may not know that baking soda can do the same thing. It doesn't work quite as well, but it can help you out in a pinch. Use a generous hand and spread evenly, breaking up any clumps. To create traction, sprinkle sand or kitty litter on top of the baking soda.

 ## WEEDS IN THE DRIVEWAY

It never ceases to amaze that weeds can somehow grow up and out of a surface as seemingly inhospitable as a driveway. While their tenacity might be admirable, the weeds are also a major source of irritation. The good news is that they're no match for vinegar. If you have a short driveway, you might simply put some vinegar in a spray bottle and spray the weeds directly. If, however, you've got a longer lane, a pump sprayer might be the faster and easier way to go.

Good to Know:
Vinegar will kill almost every plant in its path, so avoid spraying places like your lawn and garden.

 ## WEED WHACKER

Weeds also tend to pop up between sidewalk cracks, along gravel paths, and other inconvenient spots. You can use the vinegar treatment above or try a salt solution. Sprinkle the weeds with salt and then wet them with a watering can. Just like with vinegar, be careful not to get the salt on plants you want to keep or areas that you'd like to use for gardening or landscaping because it will affect the growth of future plants you place in that soil.

GARAGE AND CAR

 GARAGE OIL STAIN

It's not uncommon to have an oil spill or stain on the garage floor. To clean it up, cover the area with baking soda—it will help absorb the excess oil. Let it sit overnight, then scrub the spot well with a stiff brush moistened with water. Use a hose or bucket to rinse.

 OR TRY . . .

You can also use a salt paste to clean an oil stain.

 HEADLIGHT CLEANER

Your car's headlights and windshield can be a magnet for dead bugs, tar, salt, and other nasty things. To remove them, sprinkle a little bit of baking soda on a wet sponge and scrub away. Then rinse well and buff with a dry cloth.

  CHROME POLISH

Believe it or not, you can polish car chrome with lemon juice or vinegar. Use a soft cloth and apply either full-strength or in a 50:50 water mix. Be sure to rinse and dry well afterwards.
Bonus tip: To get chrome extra clean, scrub it first with a mixture of half baking soda, half water, then rinse.

CAR SEAT CLEANER

The next time you wash your car, don't forget about the interiors too. Sprinkle baking soda over the cloth seats, then wash the exterior of your car as usual. The baking soda will go to work on eliminating odors. Once you've finished up with the outside of the car, simply vacuum the seats, taking the baking soda and any dirt and dust with you. You may not be able to bring back that new car smell, but you can certainly have a *clean* car smell.

 ## BUMPER STICKER REMOVER

When it's time to get rid of that bumper sticker proclaiming support for your town's 2002 mayoral candidate or a cause you no longer feel so strongly about, turn to vinegar. Soak a cloth in vinegar and place it on the bumper sticker for about five minutes, which should loosen it enough so that you can scrape it off. Remove any sticky residue with a little more vinegar, or even vegetable oil. Rinse the area, then dry.

BIKES

 ## RUST REMOVER

Give your bike a little spring cleaning and remove any rust spots. Mix together one part lemon juice to three parts salt, and scrub away spots on the handlebars, frame, and rims. Rinse with water and buff with a soft cloth.

THE MANY USES OF CASTILE SOAP

Castile soap should be an essential component of every green cleaner's toolkit. It's a vegetable-based soap—often made from olive, hemp, and coconut oils—that is gentle and completely biodegradable. This simple soap comes in both bar and liquid forms, though it's the liquid version that is easiest to adapt to household uses (other than bathing). Unscented varieties are the mildest, but it also comes in lavender, rose, tea tree, almond, peppermint, and other natural scents.

Reduce soap scum. Swap out your regular soap or body wash for castile soap. Not only will your skin thank you, but you won't have to work as hard to clean the tub and tile because castile doesn't leave the same kind of residue behind.

Wash your face. A few drops of liquid castile soap can replace your regular facial cleanser.

Mop your floor. Add about one tablespoon castile soap to one to one and a half gallons of warm water and mop your floors.

Clean marble. You can even clean sealed marble floors and countertops with highly diluted castile soap. Place a few drops of soap in a bucket of water and mop or wipe. Rinse with water and dry well.

All-purpose cleanser. Use a quarter cup castile soap in a spray bottle filled with water. If you prefer a fragrance, choose a scented soap or add a few drops of your favorite essential oil. Use to wipe down kitchens and countertops, clean bathrooms, and much more.

Dish soap. Run out of dishwashing liquid? Just add a squirt of castile soap to a sink full of hot water.

Car wash. Dissolve a few tablespoons of liquid castile soap in a bucket of warm water and wash the car.

Grease cutter. For heavy-duty cleaning, use full strength castile soap to cut through grease. Rinse well.

PETS

Cats

 CAT BOX ODORS

Sprinkle your cat's litter box regularly with baking soda to cut down on nasty odors. When you clean the box, add a thin layer of baking soda in the bottom before putting in the clean litter.

 MISSED OPPORTUNITY

If your cat missed the litter box, sprinkle the spot with baking soda to neutralize the smell.

TRAIN YOUR CAT

Every time you turn your back, your cat is on the counter or another surface where she doesn't belong. Help train her with a spray made of half water and half vinegar. Just spritz a little bit where you don't want her to go, and she'll stay away because she won't like the smell.

Good to Know:
Before spraying on upholstery or other delicate surfaces, check for colorfastness because vinegar could discolor the fabric

 ## SPRAY AWAY

Un-neutered male cats, also known as tom cats, can hang around a home, leaving an awful-smelling urine spray that seems to linger forever. Help keep these cats at bay by spraying vinegar regularly around the home. If this doesn't help, see if your town offers a free neutering program for stray cats; that's the best "fix," so to speak, for this situation.

Good to Know:
Since vinegar will kill plant life, avoid spraying directly on landscaping, gardens, or yards.

Dogs

FLEA-FREE BATH

For an all-natural flea treatment, add one cup of apple cider vinegar to your dog's bath water. The vinegar will also help deodorize the dog's fur. As a topical treatment, you can put one tablespoon apple cider vinegar in a spray bottle filled with water and spray the dog's fur regularly. Ask your vet first whether this would work for your dog.

 ## CANINE DRY SHAMPOO

Just like humans, dogs can benefit from a dry shampoo. Baking soda will absorb odors and oils, making your dog smell better. Sprinkle it onto his coat, and comb it through to remove it. (You may also want to ruffle his fur a bit with a towel.) Since this tip can get a little messy, it's best to do it outside.

 ## NIX THE DOG SMELL

Help eliminate that stinky dog smell by adding baking soda to the water the next time you give your dog a bath. Dissolve one quarter cup in the tub and wash the dog as usual.

Pet Toys

 ## FOR CLEAN PET TOYS

Pet toys can get covered in saliva, dirt, hair, and whatever else might be lurking on your floor or in your yard. To clean the toys, soak them in a bath of baking soda and water. A quarter cup of baking soda dissolved in a sink full of hot water should do it. Rinse well and let the toys dry.

  ## OR TRY . . .

Vinegar will also deodorize and clean pet toys. Mix together one half cup vinegar and two cups water, and clean the toys with a sponge soaked in this solution. Be sure to rinse the toys well after you clean them, so there's no lingering vinegar aroma on them.

Try This Twist: If you've got some extra lemon juice around, you can substitute lemon juice for the vinegar.

 ## PET BED CARE

If you can't machine wash your pet's bed, keep odors to a minimum by sprinkling it regularly with baking soda. Brush it over the surface to evenly distribute, then let it sit for an hour. Sweep the baking soda, hair, and other dirt using the upholstery attachment on a canister vacuum. Hang it outside for an afternoon in the sun to freshen it up even more. If the bed is machine washable, toss one quarter to one half cup baking soda in the machine along with the laundry detergent.

 ## DISH WASHER

Wash your pet's food and water dishes in a baking soda and water mix. One part baking soda to four parts hot water will get them clean. For stuck-on food and other spots, apply baking soda directly to the area and scrub with a sponge.

 ## OR TRY . . .

Baking soda not strong enough? Disinfect the dishes with vinegar.

Pet Accidents

FOR HARD-FLOOR SURFACES

Your furry friend might leave you some unpleasant surprises on the floor from time to time. After you've wiped up the mess, cover the area with vinegar to disinfect and deodorize. Wait a few minutes, then mop up the vinegar with plain water.

FOR CARPETS

After cleaning up a pet stain on the carpet, sprinkle the damp rug with baking soda to deodorize. When the rug dries, simply vacuum up the baking soda and the smell should be gone.

FIGHTING PESTS NATURALLY

Bay leaves. Many different pests are turned off by bay leaves, those large dry leaves used to flavor sauces. Scatter a few around your pantry to fight weevils, pantry beetles, roaches, and more. Swap the bay leaves with new ones every few months for best results.

Basil. Flies and mosquitoes don't like the sweet smell of basil. Place or plant basil where these pests tend to congregate and you'll send them elsewhere.

Catnip. This herb will make your cat as happy as it will make mosquitoes unhappy.

Chalk. Draw a line with chalk to keep ants from entering your home.

Cinnamon. Cinnamon is a warm, comforting spice—unless you're an ant. Sprinkle cinnamon where ants tend to enter the home, or dab those areas with cinnamon oil.

Coffee grounds. Indoors or out, used coffee ground deter ants.

Hot Sauce. Guess who can't stand the heat? Roaches.

Lavender. Instead of using nasty mothballs in your closet, try lavender. Either dried or as an essential oil, it keeps your clothes smelling fresh and clothes moths away from your sweaters. You can dab cedar oil around the closet as well.

Marigolds. Mosquitoes don't like the smell of marigolds one bit, so be sure to plant plenty of them if you're in a mosquito-prone area or if you like to entertain outdoors on summer evenings—the time you're most likely to be eaten alive by the little buzzing beasties. Gardeners, take note: certain varieties of marigolds also repel troublesome whiteflies that may collect and feed on the undersides of leaves.

Peppermint oil. It's said mice don't enjoy the refreshing scent of peppermint quite as much as their human counterparts, so it's often recommended to place cotton balls soaked in peppermint oil around the places of your home where you've seen the critters. At the same time, you might look for holes and cracks where they're entering your home and patch the spots with steel wool—or a more permanent solution.

PEST CONTROL

 ## STOP THE ANTS FROM MARCHING

Ants won't cross over lemon juice, so if you find that you've got an army of them coming into your home, stop them by spreading lemon on windowsills, in doorways, or other points of entry.

Good to Know:
Do a patch test first to make sure lemon juice won't damage the paint or other surface you're using it on.

  ## VINEGAR SPRAY FOR ANTS

Spray ants with a mixture of vinegar and water to kill them. You can also clean surfaces with vinegar and water or lemon and water to make them ant-unfriendly.

 ## A ONE-TWO PUNCH FOR ROACHES

A baking soda and sugar mixture can help get rid of roaches. They'll be attracted by the sugar, but the baking soda will do them in. Mix the two ingredients in equal amounts and place the powder wherever you've seen roaches—under the sink, in cabinets, near the stove.

FRUITY FRUIT FLY TRAP

If you've got a fruit fly problem in your home, you can trap the pesky insects with apple cider vinegar. Just place some vinegar in a bowl and add a quarter teaspoon dish soap and a pinch of sugar. Cover the bowl with plastic wrap and secure with a rubber band. Use a toothpick to poke a few holes in the plastic wrap, then set the bowl out where you tend to see the flies. They'll be drawn to the fruity smell of the apple cider vinegar, will fly into the bowl, and be unable to escape. The soap will help kill them as well.

Try This Twist: You can substitute an old banana for the apple cider vinegar.

 ## MAKE SILVERFISH SCRAM

Silverfish thrive in damp areas and especially love to munch on paper and boxes. You'll often find the ugly creatures running through an old box in the attic or along the bathroom wall. While they might nibble at the edges of your copy of *Jane Eyre* or your 1989 tax returns, they won't touch lemon with a ten-foot pole. Spray a mixture of lemon juice and water where you tend to see them, and they'll scram.

SPIDERS DON'T LIKE LEMONS

Don't expect a spider to drop in for a glass of lemonade anytime soon. They don't like citrus, so if you're looking to keep a certain area of your home spider-free, wipe down surfaces with lemon juice or spray it where they tend to enter your home.

- CHAPTER 4 -

DO-IT-YOURSELF BEAUTY

WHAT CAN LEMONS, salt, baking soda, and vinegar do for your beauty routine? A lot it turns out, but most importantly, they can simplify, simplify, simplify! With the tips in this chapter, you may find yourself opting for a more minimalistic approach—and even wanting to toss many of those pricey lotions and potions with paragraph-long lists of ingredients. Not only will you be able to open your medicine cabinet without having the contents fall out on top of you, but you'll also be putting fewer chemicals on your skin. (A 2009 report, for example, by Britain's *Daily Mail* revealed that the average woman puts over five hundred chemicals on her skin per day, between makeup, hair-care, and skincare products.)

Let's look at the beauty benefits of each of the magic four. While each one has special properties, there's actually some overlap, so if you're temporarily out of one, you might be able to make an easy substitution or check another section for a similar tip.

Lemons. The acid in lemons can be harnessed to exfoliate skin, bleach and lighten hair, and treat minor skin problems, among many other possibilities. As an antibacterial and astringent, it can be used to fight acne. Plus, it has a pleasing smell that's thought to boost the mood.

Salt. Sea salt and Epsom salt (for an exploration of Epsom salt, see page 207), have a wonderful detoxifying effect on the skin. Salt's coarse texture means it's an excellent exfoliant and can be used as the basis of many wonderful homemade scrubs that remove dead skin cells and promote blood circulation. It's anti-inflammatory (bye-bye, puffiness) and can soothe irritated skin. It can also help treat wounds, as anyone whose ever gotten salt in a cut can tell you.

Baking soda. The uses for baking soda in particular seem endless, and the realm of beauty is no exception. Baking soda is both antifungal and antiseptic, and it banishes odors—good properties whether you're talking about refrigerator odor or your smelly feet. Like its partners, lemons and salt, it's also good for exfoliation, but it really shines in neutralizing odors and removing buildup from hair, brushes, etc. It's also great for making bath bombs and other relaxing treats.

Vinegar. You may be understandably wary about adding vinegar to your beauty routine. (The last I checked, it still smelled like vinegar.) But the good news is that when it dries the smell goes away, and the benefits outweigh that temporary odor. Vinegar has special antibacterial and antifungal properties. It also helps balance the pH of skin, soften skin, and reduce irritation. It can neutralize odor, and like lemon, it can bleach dark spots on skin. For vinegar tips, unless otherwise specified, white or apple cider vinegar is preferred.

In this chapter, as a bonus, we'll also look at some other natural beauty all-stars, like olive oil, honey, tea tree oil, and the newest trendy darling, coconut oil, and offer a few suggestions for how those items can be added to your routine.

In general, though, a word of caution: skip a tip if your skin is cracked or broken or if you're sensitive to any of the ingredients. Common sense says to keep lemon juice and vinegar (or any substance, really) away from the immediate eye area.

SKIN

Scrubs

 SCRUB AWAY DEAD SKIN

Use the power of lemons to boost exfoliation. Juice two lemons and combine with enough cornmeal (about one third of a cup) to make a damp, sandy texture. Before your next shower, rub the mixture into your skin for a few minutes to remove dead skin cells. Rinse to reveal softer, smoother skin.

 BASIC SEA SALT SCRUB (AND VARIATIONS)

For rough spots on hands, feet, and elbows, try this salt scrub. Put a quarter cup sea salt in a small bowl, and slowly start to stir in a little bit of olive oil until you get a damp paste (about one to two tablespoons should usually do it). Rub into the affected areas for a minute or so, then rinse. You can also double or triple this basic recipe and keep the leftovers in an airtight jar in the refrigerator—or use a fancy jar and give as holiday gifts!

Try This Twist: The variations on this basic scrub are endless. Mix in some crushed lavender, rosemary, or lemon zest. Substitute coconut or apricot kernel oil for the olive oil. Try a mood-boosting essential oil, like peppermint, eucalyptus, jasmine, or lemon. The sky's the limit to your creativity.

LEMON-SUGAR SCRUB

This delicious-smelling scrub rivals more expensive department store alternatives. Mix together a quarter cup lemon juice with a half cup sugar and two teaspoons olive oil until you get a sandy mixture. Rub onto clean skin, then rinse. The lemon and sugar will help exfoliate the skin, while the small amount of olive oil will moisturize and leave your skin silky smooth.

BODY BUFFER

For serious exfoliation, try a similar Epsom salt–coconut oil scrub. In a small bowl, mix together one cup Epsom salts with one quarter cup coconut oil. Use this on feet, elbows, hands, or anywhere you need to smooth away rough spots.

BOOST YOUR MOISTURIZER

To make your skin look great, mix in a few drops of apple cider vinegar to your regular moisturizer. Apply just after toweling off when the skin can best absorb it. The acidity in vinegar will help tighten your pores, making skin appear younger, and the moisturizer will leave your skin silky smooth.

 ## SALT AND HONEY FACIAL MASK

Mix together two teaspoons salt with two teaspoons honey and apply to clean skin. Leave ten minutes, then rinse off. This mask is great for combination skin because the salt draws out excess oil, while the antibacterial honey moisturizes.

 ## SALT FACIAL SCRUB

Instead of buying a separate facial scrub, make your regular cleanser do double duty. Add a quarter teaspoon Epsom salt to your cleanser before washing your face, and it will cleanse your pores, remove dead skin cells, and leave your skin looking brighter.

 ## SECRET FACIAL SCRUB

For a result that rivals high-priced facial scrubs, place a little baking soda in your palm and add water to form a loose paste. Rub in circles on clean skin, then rinse. You'll be surprised at how well the little granules buff your skin. Follow up with your favorite moisturizer. Repeat once every week or two. (More often could cause irritation.)
Try This Twist: Use equal parts honey and baking soda.

Masks

 VINEGAR-HONEY MASK

If you have dry skin, give this moisturizing facial mask a try. Mix together one tablespoon honey with one and a half teaspoons apple cider vinegar. Spread on clean skin. Let sit fifteen minutes, then rinse. The honey helps soothe and moisturize, while the vinegar has a balancing and calming effect.

Try This Twist: Really dry skin? Mix in an egg yolk for extra moisturizing power.

 LEMON AND EGG MASK

If you have oily, acne-prone skin, or if you simply want to tighten the appearance of pores, give this lemon, egg white, and honey facial a try. Whisk together one egg white with two teaspoons freshly squeezed lemon juice and one teaspoon honey (for extra benefits, splurge and use Manuka honey). Apply to face and neck with a cotton ball and allow to dry, about fifteen to twenty minutes. Rinse with cool water. The egg white tones and repairs skin, making it look more youthful; the lemon juice acts as a blemish-fighting astringent, and the antibacterial honey adds needed moisture.

FAVORITE HOME REMEDIES: BAKING SODA

Baking soda, or sodium bicarbonate, occurs naturally but is usually manufactured. It has a great range of remedial uses, but it's a good idea to check with your doctor before trying anything new, especially if you're taking medication or suffer from any condition.

Baking soda is an antacid. It says so right on the back of the box, but you may never have tried it. Baking soda is alkaline, so if you're having heartburn, it may be just the thing to tame it. Dissolve one half teaspoon in one half cup water and take every two hours.

Good to Know: There are a number of cautions when it comes to using baking soda as an antacid, so it's best to check with your doctor first. I won't cover all of the concerns here, but you should read the warnings and directions on the box very carefully, because it's not for everyone, including children and those on a low-sodium diet, as well as those with certain medical conditions or taking certain drugs. You shouldn't take baking soda on a full stomach either, and you should never take more than the recommended amount.

Replace your deodorant. Baking soda fights odor everywhere else in your home, why not your armpits too? (Note that some people find this causes skin irritation.)

Treat bites and stings. Make a paste of baking soda and water and apply it to a bug bite or sting for relief.

Whiten your teeth. Just dip your toothbrush in baking soda and brush for whiter teeth. For extra cleaning power, mix together a paste of hydrogen peroxide and baking soda and use that instead of your regular toothbrush for occasional whitening. Be sure to spit and not swallow either of these ingredients, and ask your dentist if this tip would work for you.

Toners & Cleansers

TONE UP

Swap out your regular facial toner for this vinegar-based version. For oily skin, mix together a quarter cup vinegar and a quarter cup water in a small jar, and shake to combine. Soak a cotton ball in the mixture and apply to clean skin to tighten pores and remove impurities.

STEAM CLEAN

This lemon facial couldn't be simpler, and as a bonus, the fresh scent will boost your mood. First, remove all makeup and clean your face and neck. Next, pour boiling water in a large bowl, then add some fresh lemon slices. To increase the lemon aroma, you could even add a drop of lemon essential oil. Place your face over the bowl and cover your head with a towel. (Be sure that the steam is not too hot first.) Do this for about five minutes, then rinse your face with cool water and relax.

LEMON CUCUMBER TONER

Here's another toning mask for oily skin. In a blender, puree a quarter cup lemon juice and a quarter cup cucumber. Dab the mixture on skin and allow to sit for five minutes, before rinsing off with cool water.

Blemishes

 GET BACK AT BACNE

Back acne, better known as "bacne," can be annoying and embarrassing. Have a friend or partner dip a cotton ball in white or apple cider vinegar and apply it to the affected sections of the back. The acidity will dry out the blemish and balance the skin's pH.

Bonus Tip: You can also use this tip for acne on the face or other parts of the body.

 NATURAL PIMPLE CREAM

To get those pimples packing, in your palm mix together a little bit of baking soda with enough hydrogen peroxide to make a paste. Apply it directly to the pimple before bed. Repeat every evening until it diminishes.

 BANISH A BLEMISH

Want to pop that pimple? Wait and try this simple treatment instead. Mix together a little bit of baking soda with enough honey to make a paste. The baking soda will help reduce the pimple, while the honey has antibacterial properties. Apply it to the pimple for ten minutes, then rinse.

GOOD-BYE BLACKHEADS

To treat blackheads, apply straight lemon juice with a cotton ball before going to bed. Repeat for a few days until you see results.
Bonus Tip: Lemon juice can also help dry up a pimple more quickly.

 ## LIGHTEN UP SCARS!

Lemon can help lighten scars, blotches, and dark spots on the skin. In a small bowl, mix together one part lemon juice, one part honey, and two parts plain yogurt. Apply the mixture to the spots for about ten minutes, then rinse. Repeat regularly for best effects, and discontinue if irritation occurs.

 ## AID FOR AGE SPOTS

Age spots, sometimes called liver spots, occur as a result of sun exposure. (The liver has nothing to do with them, and they can strike at any age.) They can be tough to lighten, but lemon juice is thought to be of help. Dab some of the juice on the spot every day for a month or so, but be sure to stop if it causes irritation. In the meantime, don't forget to wear plenty of sunblock.

 ## LIGHTEN AGE SPOTS

Age spots are stubborn, but you can dry dabbing them daily with apple cider vinegar. If it works for you, it may take weeks before you see results. In the meantime, discontinue if you experience any irritation.

Dry Skin

  ## LEMON ELBOW REAMER

In a hurry, but need to get rid of rough spots on elbows? Try this speedy solution. Cut a lemon in half and sprinkle it with plenty of kosher salt. Then, hold your elbow over the sink and use the lemon half as a sort of reamer on your elbow. The combination of the acid and the abrasive properties of the salt will smooth away rough patches. Repeat with the other elbow, then rinse and apply a moisturizer.

Try This Twist: Use lime if you're out of lemon.

 ## WINTER SKIN REMEDY

Soothe dry winter hands and feet with this comforting and moisturizing skin mask. Mix together two teaspoons coconut oil and two teaspoons honey with half teaspoon lemon juice. Make sure all ingredients are well blended (if the coconut oil is too firm, try softening it in the microwave for a few seconds). Massage into the hands and feet—and any other rough spots. After ten to fifteen minutes, rinse to reveal smoother, more moisturized skin.

FOR CORNS AND CALLUSES

The acid in lemon could just be the thing to soften up corns and calluses on your feet. Before turning in at night, place a small slice of lemon (or even a cotton ball soaked in lemon juice) over the spot. Cover with a bandage. Remove in the morning, rinse, and then dry the area.

SOFTEN UP

To soften rough patches on feet, elbows, and hands, mix together equal parts baking soda and lemon juice to make a paste. Apply to affected area and let sit a few minutes, before rinsing away. Follow up with a good moisturizer to keep the softening going.

Lips

  FOR SMOOTH LIPS

Use the baking soda–lemon mixture on the previous page to exfoliate lips. Rub on lips for twenty to thirty seconds, then rinse and apply your favorite lip balm.

 LIP SCRUB

If your lips are flaky and dry, you may need to remove some of those dead skin cells so that moisturizer can be absorbed. Mix together a teaspoon of salt (sea, kosher, or Epsom) along with a teaspoon of coconut oil. Rub the mixture in a circular motion on dry lips for a minute or so then wipe away the excess to reveal healthier-looking, smoother lips.

BREATH

  ## SIMPLY FRESH BREATH

This easy, effective mouthwash will only cost you pennies. Salt and baking soda can tag team to banish bad breath. Dissolve one half teaspoon salt and one half teaspoon baking soda in water. Swish and gargle with the mixture for thirty to sixty seconds, then spit.

Good to Know:
Ask a doctor first if you're on a low-sodium diet.

 ## BREATH FRESHENER

If lunch left your breath feeling less than fresh, try sucking on a lemon wedge, or squeeze the juice of one lemon in a cup of water. If that's too sour of a solution, dip the wedge into sugar before sucking on it. Since lemon juice is an acid, save this tip for occasional use.

TEETH

 ## FOR PEARLIER WHITES

To get whiter teeth, mix together one teaspoon finely ground sea salt and three teaspoons baking soda, being sure to break up any lumps. Dip a wet toothbrush in the mixture and brush as usual, then rinse well. Be sure to check with your dentist, but you should be able to use this mixture once a week.

Good to Know: Note that it is not recommended for those with sensitive teeth or gums..

 ## WHITER, BRIGHTER TEETH

You can also use baking soda and peroxide as a toothpaste. Mix together one teaspoon baking soda with one half teaspoon hydrogen peroxide, and transfer the paste to your toothbrush. Brush as usual, and rinse thoroughly. As long as you don't have sensitive teeth or gums, you can use this treatment once a week.

 ## FRESHEN UP RETAINERS AND MOUTHGUARDS

Teenagers who use mouthguards for sports or wear orthodontic retainers can soak them for thirty minutes in a cup of water with a tablespoon of dissolved baking soda. It will help eliminate odors and keep them clean. Just rinse with water before using.

WHAT'S THE DEAL WITH COCONUT OIL?

Long demonized for its high saturated fat content, coconut oil has been experiencing a resurgence in popularity in recent years. Now if you visit any Whole Foods or health-food store, you'll find it right alongside heart-healthy extra virgin olive oil and organic expeller-pressed canola oil. It's touted for its ability to turn into flaky piecrusts, fluffy icings, delicious stir-fries (particularly Thai and Indian dishes), and more. It makes a great substitute for butter for vegans, those who can't eat dairy for other reasons, or those who simply want to experiment in the kitchen. In terms of

its health benefits, it's extolled for everything from weight loss and lower cholesterol to regulating blood sugar and strengthening bones. Oil pulling, the ancient Ayurvedic technique of swishing oil (particularly the coconut variety) in your mouth for up to twenty minutes a day, is thought to whiten teeth, fight gingivitis, improve breath, and even alleviate headaches and sleep problems.

So why the 180-degree shift from demon to darling? As it turns out, according to a 2011 article in the *New York Times* by Melissa Clark, many of the early studies on coconut oil were done with the hydrogenated (read: trans fat) version of the oil, and scientists pretty much universally agree that trans fat is bad for us. Also, this highly processed version lost many of the beneficial qualities of its virgin counterpart, such as its antioxidants and fatty acids. And finally, while coconut oil is indeed 90 percent saturated fat (butter, by contrast, has 64 percent saturated fat, and lard 40 percent) scientists now have a more nuanced understanding of these fats and believe that the *kind* of saturated fat found in coconut oil may have some beneficial qualities, including a possible ability to boost good cholesterol (HDL). While this doesn't mean that we should all run out and consume huge quantities of the stuff, it does mean that we can incorporate it in moderation into a healthy diet in place of other fats.

While scientists sort out the health claims, let's look at a few of the best ways you can incorporate coconut oil in your beauty routine. It's a fabulous moisturizer, has a pleasant aroma, blends well with other ingredients, and its unique texture (solid at room temperature) makes it a good option for mixing up your own DIY body creams. Stick with raw virgin coconut oil (preferably organic) for these tips.

Dry skin. Apply straight coconut oil to dry skin after a shower. Consider keeping a small jar of it in your bag for on-the-go moisture. Mix with a few drops of essential oil in for a fragrant treat. It's great on rough spots, like heels, elbows, and hands.

Deep conditioner. After shampooing, apply a nickel-sized amount of coconut oil to your hair in place of your regular conditioner. Let sit for twenty to thirty minutes, then rinse.

Makeup remover. The oil in coconut breaks down stubborn makeup. Swap your regular remover for a few days to try.

Frizz fighter. Instead of using a silicone-based anti-frizz product, just rub a dab of coconut oil between your palms and then tame those flyaways. Not only will your hair be sleek and smooth, but you'll also give it some much-needed moisture.

Body scrub. Try this amazingly scented vanilla–coconut oil sugar scrub. With a hand mixer, blend together one half cup coconut oil, one cup sugar, and one half teaspoon vanilla (or an essential oil). Also see "Body Buffer," page 182.

HAIR

Color

LOCK IN HAIR COLOR

If you dye your hair at home, do a final rinse of one cup white vinegar with two cups water before rinsing with cold water. It will help your hair color last longer.

HAIR HIGHLIGHTER

If you'd like to lighten your hair naturally, try that old childhood favorite: lemon juice and sunshine. Since lemon juice can dry out your hair, in this updated recipe, you'll add a little bit of olive oil as a moisturizer. You'll need about one half cup lemon juice (from three to four lemons), one half teaspoon ground cinnamon (which boosts the lightening properties of lemon juice), one cup water, and two  teaspoons olive oil. Place all ingredients in a spray bottle, shake to combine, and spray on desired sections of hair until damp. Now head outside and let the sun do its part. (Wearing sunscreen, of course.) After about an hour or so, shampoo your hair to remove the mixture and condition well. The results will be subtle but noticeable. If you'd like to go lighter, repeat again in about a week, but stop if the lemon starts to become too drying.

Volume

 ## ADD BODY TO HAIR

Supercharge your regular shampoo with baking soda. Mix about a half teaspoon into your normal palm-full of shampoo. Lather and rinse as usual. The baking soda will help eliminate build up from styling products, conditioners, and even hard water, so your hair will have more body and your scalp will feel cleaner.

 ## PUMP UP THE VOLUME

Dry winter days may leave your hair limper than a wet noodle, but Epsom salts can supercharge your conditioner to give you enviable volume. Mix together one teaspoon Epsom salts and one teaspoon conditioner, and massage through clean, wet hair. Wait fifteen minutes, then rinse and style as usual.

 ## BEACHY WAVES WITHOUT THE BEACH

Have you ever noticed how great your hair looks after a day at the beach? Despite being tousled and windblown, your normally troublesome locks now have effortless, to-die-for waves. It's the salt air and water that does it, and many sea salt sprays on the market can help you recreate that beach-perfect look everyday. But it's just as easy—and much cheaper—to make your own. Stir together one and a half cups hot water, one tablespoon sea salt, one teaspoon Epsom salts, one tablespoon coconut oil, and one teaspoon hair conditioner. (Use a leave-in conditioner if you can.) Make sure the salts are fully dissolved and the coconut oil and conditioner evenly distributed. Transfer mixture to a clean spray bottle and shake well before each use. If you wish, you can even add a drop or two of your favorite essential oil to give it a pleasing fragrance.

Shampoo & Conditioner

 ## NO 'POO?

If you've spent any time on natural blogs on the internet, you'll probably have noticed a number of thrifty, earthy individuals extolling the myriad virtues of swapping out your regular shampoo and conditioner for—wait for it—a baking soda shampoo with apple cider vinegar rinse. Many people go through a bad-hair break-in period, but come out on the other side claiming it makes hair softer, shinier, less frizzy, and more manageable. Plus, it's a more natural alternative to commercial shampoos. Here's the process if you'd like to give it a try and see if it works for you. First, mix together  one quarter cup baking soda with two cups water. Stir to dissolve. Apply to mixture to the scalp and scrub, then rinse it out. Follow up with a quarter cup apple cider vinegar mixed with the same amount of water. Pour over your head, massage gently through, and rinse immediately. You can play with these measurements until you get a dilution you're happy with over time. (If done properly, your hair should not have a residual vinegar aroma.) You can also mix up larger quantities and keep the bottles in your shower. Just stir or shake before using to recombine.

 ## PRODUCT BUILDUP

To eliminate product and scalp buildup, mix together one tablespoon white vinegar with two cups water. Shampoo and condition hair as usual, then pour this mixture over the hair. No need to rinse it out.

FLAKE FIGHTER

If you're suffering from stubborn dandruff, you might try this salt treatment before your next shampoo. Take a few tablespoons of coarse salt and rub into your scalp for five minutes to help dislodge flakes. Rinse, then shampoo and condition as usual.

DRY SHAMPOO SUBSTITUTE

You've probably seen those dry shampoos that are all the rage, but there's no need to spend money on them. Instead, work a little baking soda into your roots, wait a few minutes, then comb your hair to remove it. It will absorb excess oils, allowing you to stretch out time between washes.

 ## CONDITION AND ADD SHINE TO HAIR

To make hair shine, follow up your regular shampoo with a white or cider vinegar rinse. Mix together one part vinegar to two parts water and pour over clean, wet hair, then rinse.

 ## DO AWAY WITH DANDRUFF

To treat dandruff, mix together one part lemon juice with two parts water. After shampooing, rub the mixture into the scalp and rinse. Since lemon can be drying, be sure to follow up with a good conditioner. You can repeat every other day for a week.

 ## DUST OFF DANDRUFF

Apple cider vinegar is considered to help reduce dandruff. You can apply it straight to the scalp or mix with an equal amount of olive oil to add moisture. Rub in for several minutes and then rinse well. Shampoo as usual.

SEA SALT SHAMPOO

You may have seen shampoos with sea salt that boast their ability to soften, add body, and shine to hair. To get the same effect without the sticker shock, just mix a tablespoon of sea salt into your regular shampoo bottle.

Bonus Tip: Or, for a quick fix for oily hair or scalp buildup, mix together equal parts salt and shampoo, and apply to hair, paying special attention to the roots and scalp.

 ## POOL-HAIR CARE

You may love to swim, but your hair begs to differ. Over time, chlorinated water can make your locks look dull and discolored, especially if you're blond. To counteract the harsh effect, dissolve one tablespoon baking soda in two cups water and pour over your hair after you've been in the pool. Then shampoo and condition as usual.

 ## DE-GUNK THAT HAIRBRUSH

Remove buildup from hairbrushes and combs by soaking it in a small basin of warm water mixed with one tablespoon dissolved baking soda. Then rinse and allow to dry completely before storing.

Bonus Tip: Clean your makeup brushes this way too!

TEA TREE OIL

Tea tree oil has many uses in a natural home tool-kit, not least of which is its beauty benefits, particularly for those with oily or acne-prone skin. This essential oil is distilled from the leaves of a tree native to Australia and is believed to have antibacterial and antifungal properties when used on the skin. Some early studies have even shown effectiveness in fighting MRSA, a potentially deadly bacterial infection. In daily use, it's considered to be as effective in fighting acne as benzoyl peroxide, but with less skin irritation. You can also try it for athlete's foot and nail fungus. It has a camphor-like odor, which some people like, but others may find bothersome.

If you have sensitive skin or a condition like eczema or rosacea, tea tree oil might aggravate it. It's always a smart idea to check with your doctor before using any new product (even a natural one), especially if you're taking any medication. Also, tea tree oil should never be swallowed as it's toxic when taken internally.

If you'd like to try it, look for fair-trade versions, and make sure the bottle you buy is tinted or dark for maximum effectiveness.

Zap zits. Apply 5 percent tea tree oil to pimple every night before bed.
Remove makeup. Mix together a quarter cup olive oil and eight to ten drops of tea tree oil. Apply with a cotton ball or pad in circular motions. Follow up with your regular cleanser and moisturizer.
Fight dandruff. Add a drop or two of tea tree oil to your shampoo the next time you wash your hair.
Fungus fighter. The next time you're giving yourself a manicure or pedicure, mix in a few drops of tea tree oil in your regular moisturizer, and massage into cuticles. (Or add a few drops to some coconut oil for an easy antifungal moisturizer.)

NAILS

 POWER UP YOUR NAIL POLISH

Extend the life of your next at-home manicure with vinegar. After grooming your nails, but before adding polish, dip a cotton ball in vinegar and swipe each nail with it. Allow to dry, then add your polish of choice. The idea is that vinegar removes any oils, moisture, and residue from the nail, so that the color adheres better and lasts longer.

 FOR YOUR NAIL NEEDS

Lemon can work well as a treatment for the nails.
Try soaking your fingers in a mixture of lemon and water to soften cuticles and whiten dull nails. To eliminate the dirt underneath nails, dig your fingertips into a half of a lemon and move them back and forth to dislodge the grime.

  BRIGHTEN NAILS

There's nothing more delightful than a perfect manicure, but the downside is the yellowish cast nails can take on over time as a result of wearing polish. Use the natural bleaching power of baking soda and lemon to help. Measure out a tablespoon or so of baking soda and squeeze in enough fresh lemon juice to make a paste. Rub it into clean, polish-free nails. Rinse after ten minutes for brighter nails.

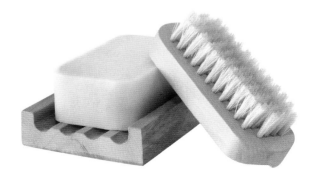

 ## DISLODGE DIRT

Dirt under your nails? Clean them up with baking soda. Mix together two parts water to one part baking soda. Use a nailbrush or even a clean toothbrush to help scrub the solution under your nails, then rinse.

CUTICLE HELPER

A loose paste of baking soda and water can help soften cuticles. Soak for five minutes, then push back cuticles. Rub any remaining paste over your hands to help aid in exfoliation.

BATHS

 ## A BETTER BATH

To help alleviate itchy skin, add three quarters of a cup white or apple cider vinegar to warm running bath water. Soak for fifteen to twenty minutes for relief. It helps balance skin's natural pH.

Bonus Tip: It's great for sore muscles.

 ## EPSOM SALT BATH

An Epsom salt bath is a classic for a reason: it works. For sore muscles or body aches or simply to relax the body at the end of a stressful day, dissolve two cups Epsom salts in running water, and soak for fifteen to twenty minutes for relief. (It's also thought to help contribute to a good night's sleep.)

Try This Twist: Want to spice it up? Mix together one cup Epsom salt with a few drops of your favorite fragrance or essential oil.

BATH BOOSTER

For a soothing bath, add one half cup fine sea salt along with two or three drops of your favorite essential oil to the running water.

 ## DETOXIFYING BATH

A simple baking soda bath can detoxify and soften skin, helping calm irritation and itchiness. Dissolve one half cup baking soda into warm bathwater. Soak for approximately twenty minutes.

Bonus Tip: Baking soda also deodorizes skin, making this a great summertime bath.

EPSOM SALT

Not a true salt, Epsom is magnesium sulfate, and it may be best known in its role as that box your grandmother kept under her sink and touted as a cure for everything from constipation to sore muscles. Turns out Grandma was right.

Named after a spring in England where it was first discovered, Epsom salt is a naturally occurring substance. When the salts are dissolved in a bath, the body can absorb much-needed magnesium through the skin, which not only relieves muscular pain, but can actually help boost one's mood (through its interaction with serotonin).

FIZZY BATH BOMBS

Have you ever used one of those fizzy bath bombs? Would you be surprised to learn that the main ingredient is baking soda? Baking soda, along with citric acid, is what makes it fizz, and they're quite easy to make. Mix together one cup baking soda, one half cup citric acid (available online if you can't find a local source), and one half cup cornstarch in a large bowl until well blended. Now comes the fun part. Add in a few drops of your favorite essential oil, perhaps about a half teaspoon  total, along with a few drops of food coloring (optional). Finally, drizzle in a few teaspoons of sweet almond oil or apricot kernel oil, just enough so that the mixture starts to hold together. Transfer to molds and allow to dry for several days before using. Not only will you love using them in your bath, but you can also give them as gifts.

Try This Twist: If you're not concerned about forming them into pretty bath bombs, you can just mix up the dry ingredients, add a few drops of essential oils, and then scoop a quarter cup of the loose mixture into your bath.

HONEY DO

Honey is delicious, of course, but it's also a powerhouse in so many other ways. Eating local honey may help allergy sufferers. A spoonful can help soothe a cough. Spread as a thin layer on the skin and covered with a bandage, it can help heal minor scrapes and bruises. Honey is rich in antioxidants, particularly polyphenols. It's antibacterial and anti-inflammatory, and what's more, there's even an FDA-approved medical honey used for wounds and burns. For consumers, the wonderful and medicinal Manuka honey from New Zealand is available in most health-food stores and is considered to have higher antibiotic/antibacterial properties than regular honey. It's on the pricey side, but might be worth the splurge if you want to add a little natural luxury to your beauty routine. (Fancy spas sometimes offer Manuka honey facials.) No matter which honey you choose, you're in for a sweet treat, though for best results, choose a raw honey. (Just a reminder that honey should never be given to babies under a year old.)

Anti-inflammatory mask. Mix together two tablespoons honey, one egg, and two to three tablespoons pulverized oats. It should be a thick paste. (Add more honey or oats if needed.) Apply to freshly cleansed face for fifteen minutes, then rinse.

Exfoliating anti-aging mask. Mix together two tablespoons honey with two teaspoons of milk. Apply to clean skin, let sit for ten to fifteen minutes, then rinse with lukewarm water.

Hair mask. In small, microwave-safe bowl, mix together three tablespoons honey with one tablespoon coconut oil and microwave for a few seconds on high, just until the mixture is warm to the touch. Apply to clean, wet hair. Rinse well after thirty minutes.

Deluxe facial. Apply pure raw Manuka honey directly to clean skin for fifteen to twenty minutes. Rinse with lukewarm water.

Milk and honey bath. Add one cup milk and one half cup honey to running bath water. Soak for fifteen to twenty minutes and relax like royalty.

FEET

 ## FOOT DEODORIZER

Stinky Feet? Epsom salt can help with that too. Dissolve one half cup Epsom salt in a small basin and soak your feet for fifteen to twenty minutes. Even if your feet don't smell, this is a great tip for those days when you're on your feet a lot and need to soothe the painful swelling. Follow up with one of those tingly peppermint moisturizers for a luxuriously relaxing treat.

 ## HELP FOR SWEATY FEET

If your feet sweat a lot, dust them with baking soda before putting on your socks and shoes. Baking soda will help keep your feet dry and keep nasty foot funguses at bay.

  ## FOOT SCRUB

After you've tried the above treatment, use this scrub to help soften those rough spots. Mix together two tablespoons white vinegar, two tablespoons honey, and enough kosher salt (or other coarse salt) to make a thick paste. Massage directly into the feet with your hands or use with your pumice to make quick work of calluses.

 ## PRE-PEDICURE TREATMENT

Before your next pedicure, soak two washcloths with white vinegar and wrap around your feet for fifteen minutes or so before rinsing. You'll find it's much easier to file calluses and rough spots with a pumice stone or foot scrubber.

PUT A STOP TO STINKY SHOES

If your feet are prone to perspiration, or even if you just want to prevent odor from ever gaining a, um, foot-hold, sprinkle some baking soda in your shoes after wearing them. It will absorb both excess moisture and odor. Just remember to shake them out before wearing them again.

 ## PEDICURE FOOT SOAK

In a small basin, mix together a quarter cup baking soda, warm water, and several drops peppermint essential oil. Allow your feet to soak for fifteen to twenty minutes, then smooth away rough patches with a pumice or foot scrubber.
Bonus Tip: Try this tip if you're prone to foot odor.

SUNBURN

 ## SUNBURN SOOTHER

Epsom salt has anti-inflammatory properties that you can harness to soothe the pain of a sunburn. Place three tablespoons Epsom salt in a spray bottle and add one cup warm water. Shake to dissolve and spray as needed on irritated skin.

 ## SUNBURN SOAK

Spent too much time in the sun? Try adding one half cup baking soda to bathwater to help relieve the pain of sunburn. Make sure the water temperature is lukewarm to cool. Repeat daily until you see improvement.

 ## SUNBURN SPRAY

Got a sunburn and don't have any aloe on hand? Vinegar is great for skin irritation. Spray mixture of one half cup vinegar and one half cup water on your skin for relief. (It will feel even better if you refrigerate it first.) While you probably won't like the odor in the moment, it will promote healing and reduce pain. Plus, the smell will go away soon enough.

BODY ODOR

 BATTLE B.O.

If you're trying to avoid the harsh chemicals and aluminum used in commercial deodorants and antiperspirants, baking soda might just be the thing for you. Mix together equal parts baking soda and cornstarch and then dust on freshly cleaned armpits. Wary about letting go of your favorite roll-on? Try it for a weekend, and ask your family to give you the smell-test.

 NATURAL DEODORANT

It may surprise you to learn that vinegar is an excellent deodorizer. You can even use it to zap body odor. Dab clean unarms with straight white vinegar and allow to dry. The vinegar smell will disappear quickly, and you'll have odor-free pits.

Good to Know: Vinegar is not an antiperspirant, so you'll still sweat.

 SPONGE AWAY SMELLS

Similarly, if you've been sweating but don't have time for a quick shower, try this quick trick to neutralize odor. Stir together one cup water and one half cup vinegar. Wipe the smelly areas with a sponge dampened in the mixture, then rinse and pat dry.

SHAVING AIDS

 ## SOFTER SKIN AFTER SHAVING

Need an aftershave lotion? Try dabbing straight white vinegar on freshly shaved skin to give skin a real treat. The odor will dissipate, so you won't smell like salad.

 ## RAZOR BUMP REMEDY

To treat unsightly red razor bumps, apply vinegar to the area and let dry. It will calm the inflammation and soften skin.

 ## RAZOR BURN REMEDY

Suffering from razor burn? Dissolve a tablespoon of baking soda in a cup of water, and dab on the affected area with a cotton ball.

OLIVE OIL

Legend has it that the use of olive oil as a skin and hair treatment dates back to Cleopatra. Whether or not that's true, we do know that this "good fat" has so many uses other than making your food taste delicious. This chapter offers many beauty ideas for olive oil in conjunction with lemon, salt, baking soda, and vinegar. Here are a few other simple solutions to try.

Mega moisture. Rub pure olive oil into dry skin. If you've got dry heels, massage some olive oil into your feet before bed, cover with socks, and in the morning your skin will be much smoother.

Soften cuticles. Rub directly into cuticles before pushing them back.

Tame flyaways. Frizzy hair? A drop of olive oil will smooth hair and moisturize at the same time.

Shave legs. No shaving gel? No problem. Just rub a little bit of olive oil on your legs and shave as usual.

Good to Know:
This could make the tub or shower slippery, so be careful.

Super scrub. Olive oil is a natural partner in both salt- and sugar-based scrubs. It moisturizes while the sugar or salt sloughs away impurities and dead skin.

NOTES

1 "Sodium in Diet," U.S. National Library of Medicine: MedLinePlus, last modified May 13, 2014, accessed May 2, 2015, http://www.nlm.nih.gov/medlineplus/ency/article/002415.htm.

2 "A Brief History of Salt," *Time,* March 15, 1982, http://content.time.com/time/magazine/article/0,9171,925341,00.html.

3 Katherine Zeratsky, RD, LD, "What's the Difference Between Sea Salt and Table Salt?" Mayo Clinic, January 17, 2013, accessed May 2, 2015, http://www.mayoclinic.org/healthy-lifestyle/nutrition-and-healthy-eating/expert-answers/sea-salt/faq-20058512.

4 Julia Morton, "Lemon," Purdue University Center for New Crops and Plant Products, last updated May 2, 2011, accessed May 2, 2015, https://www.hort.purdue.edu/newcrop/morton/lemon.html.

5 Sarah Breckenridge, "At the Market: Lemon Varieties," FineCooking.com, accessed May 2, 2015, http://www.finecooking.com/articles/lemon-varieties.aspx.

6 Eva Sideman, "Baking Soda," How Products are Made 1, MadeHow.com, accessed May 2, 2015, http://www.madehow.com/Volume-1/Baking-Soda.html.

7 Sideman, "Baking Soda."

8 "Frequently Asked Questions," The Vinegar Institute, accessed May 2, 2015, http://www.versatilevinegar.org/faqs.html.

9 Markham Heid, "The Natural Disinfectant in Your Kitchen Right Now," Prevention.com, February 25, 2014, accessed May 2, 2015, http://www.prevention.com/health/healthy-living/vinegar-effective-household-cleaner.

10 William A. Rutala, PhD, MPH, David J. Weber, MD, MPH, et al, "Guideline for Disinfection and Sterilization in Healthcare Facilities, 2008," Centers for Disease Control and Prevention, last updated December 29, 2009, accessed May 2, 2015, http://www.cdc.gov/hicpac/Disinfection_Sterilization/3_3inactivBioAgents.html.

11 "Balsamic Vinegar," BBC GoodFood Glossary, accessed May 2, 2015, http://www.bbcgoodfood.com/glossary/balsamic-vinegar.

12 Sadie Whitelocks, "The Most Germ-Ridden Spot in Your Kitchen? Refrigerator Water Dispensers Found to Harbor 'Concerning' Levels of Bacteria," *Daily Mail Online,* May 6, 2013, http://www.dailymail.co.uk/femail/article-2320397/The-germ-ridden-spot-kitchen-Refrigerator-WATER-DISPENSERS-harbor-concerning-levels-bacteria.html.

13 "The Best Way to Sanitize Kitchen Sponges," Good Housekeeping, March 27, 2015, http://www.goodhousekeeping.com/home/cleaning/a18731/how-to-clean-a-sponge.

14 Rachel Wray Thompson, "The Best Way to Clean a Sponge—*Cook's Illustrated,*" February 5, 2010, http://www.apartmenttherapy.com/the-best-way-to-clean-a-sponge-107972.

15 Trevor V. Suslow and Linda J. Harris, "Growing Seed Sprouts at Home," Publication 8151, University of California, Division of Agriculture and Natural Resources, 2004, http://www.foodsafetysite.com/resources/word/factsheets/FSAlfalfaSprouts.pdf.

INDEX

FURTHER READING

Want even more household tips using salt, lemons, baking soda, and vinegar? Magazines like *Real Simple, Reader's Digest, Good Housekeeping*, and *Better Homes and Gardens* are good resources for innovative tips using all kinds of natural substances. Also check out websites like TheKitchn.com and ApartmentTherapy.com. Here are a few well-known books of household hints that you might enjoy.

Briggs, Margaret. *Practical Household Uses of Bicarbonate of Soda*. Leicestershire, England: Southwater, 2013.

———. Practical Household Uses of Salt. Leicestershire, England: Southwater, 2013.

———. Practical Household Uses of Vinegar. Leicestershire, England: Southwater, 2013.

Eds. of Publications International. Sunkist Lemons & More. Lincolnwood, Illinois: Publications International, Ltd., 2010.

Lansky, Vicki. *Baking Soda*. Deephaven, Minnesota: Book Peddlers, 2004.

———. *Vinegar*. Deephaven, Minnesota: Book Peddlers, 2004.

Moosbrugger, Patty. *Lemon Magic*. New York: Three Rivers Press, 1999.

———. *Solve It with Salt*. New York: Three Rivers Press, 1998.

Sandbeck, Ellen. *Organic Housekeeping*. New York: Scribner, 2006.

IMAGE CREDITS